Revised & Expanded!

Understanding The Jesus Code

Transforming Family Wounds So You, Your Family, And The Generations That Follow Can LIVE Fully Alive!

By: Carolyn M. Berghuis, MS, ND, CTN

"The glory of God is man fully alive."

- St. Irenaeus, a bishop and early Church Father

Published in the United States by Trinity Holistic Wellness, Inc.

Library of Congress Cataloging-in-Publication Data

Berghuis, Carolyn M.

Understanding the Jesus Code: Transforming Family Wounds So You, Your Family, And The Generations That Follow Can LIVE Fully Alive!/ Carolyn M. Berghuis.

Pages cm

Includes biographical references.

ISBN: 9781730872228

1. Forgiveness – Jesus 2. Emotions – spiritual aspects 3. Healing – Christian aspects

www.CarolynBerghuis.com

DEDICATION

To my husband, Scott L. Berghuis, who has stood by my side supporting me through the great times and the challenging times. Life would not be complete without you. I will forever be your Eve and you will forever by my Adam.

To Jesus Christ who tenderly holds me in his sacred heart, helping me as I travel through this world enveloped in his love, grace, and mercy.

Contents

« Introduction »

From Brokenness to Wholeness, the Choice Is Ours to Make

*2 Corinthians 9:8 - And God is able to provide you
with every blessing in abundance, so that you may
always have enough of everything and may provide
in abundance for every good work.*

While in our hearts we yearn for prosperity, happiness, and peace, many never experience the fullness of life they desire, and it's time for this to change. A quick look at the world today and we see individuals not meeting their full God-given potential—brokenhearted, unfulfilled dreams, and broken families. We witness patterns passed down from one generation to the next that limit happiness. Even though we are all born into a family all too often we feel alone. Out of this loneliness we turn to the world for love and comfort only to find greater heartache and challenges. Families are suffering, families are under attack, and as a result, society is experiencing anguish because we are not reaching the fullness of life God has for us.

Since you have picked up this book, I assume you are either seeking to break through and reach the fullness of your God-given potential, you are seeking to heal your own brokenheartedness, or you are a healer seeking to find a way to help those who need your care, wisdom, and guidance. Regardless of why this book ended up in your hands, it is my hope and prayer that you break through and experience happiness, peace, and prosperity beyond your wildest dreams.

While there is certainly profound human pain in the world today, we are a people of hope, fortitude, and goodness. The human person is a survivor and we continually seek our heart's desire. A cursory review of world history shows miraculous endeavors accomplished by mankind. However, in spite of man's great achievements, we must also acknowledge that we live in a world where good and bad coexist in humanity. Joy is interwoven with sorrow, prosperity coexists with poverty, good is found within heartache, and love blooms amidst hate.

For all the bad in the world, we must be ever mindful of the fact that we live in miraculous times! Many Christian leaders today speak of unity, they seek to build bridges, and they seek to support the healing of today's family and individuals in a way many have never witnessed in today's church. Our current Roman Catholic Pope, Pope Francis, has captured the hearts of billions across the world as he reveals to mankind the power of forgiveness, acceptance, and love. We see world religious leaders engage in interfaith dialogue as they speak of compassion, understanding, and unity. Yes, we are attempting to heal our hidden wounds and limitations so that we can experience the abundance, happiness, and peace we were created for and this is cause for great celebration!

However, while there is real change happening in the fabric of the world, it is those individuals who come together in the spirit of love, forgiveness, and acceptance who will experience the fullness of life. Each and every one of us is called to participate in this journey and we are all invited to use our free will to choose participation. It is my hope that throughout this book, you will come to understand your part in this plan so that you too can be a part of today's transformation movement. We can all make a difference. However, the journey, while worth taking, is not for the faint of heart. The journey will be full of bumps along the way as we experience the manifestation of our soul's desire for happiness and wholeness. We are all created in the image of God, and with this comes a promise, a promise of eternal life with God himself. However, we must first choose him because to not choose God places us outside the boundless gift of his grace. And it is inside this grace, my friends, where all the good things happen!

> We are all created in the image of God, and with this comes a promise, a promise of eternal life with God himself.

Isaiah 65:20 - "No more shall there be in it an infant that lives but a few days, or an old person who does not live out a lifetime: for one who dies at a hundred years will be considered a youth, and one who falls short of a hundred will be considered accursed."

You see, from our conception, we were created to live an eternal lifetime with God. Sadly, looking around, too many of God's children are falling short and missing out on an amazing life. Even in God's churches, we find multitudes living lives that fall short of the fullness God has for them. Take a good look around the next time you are at your place of worship. How many individuals do you see who are fully happy and full of life? You know, individuals who exude the Christ light from deep within for all to see, those who are the living essence of love itself? My guess is you can't name many. This has got to stop. The time is now for God's children to step into their full blessing.

How do we change this trajectory and step into our blessing? After all, God has made some rather amazing promises to those who follow him. Well, it's going to be a process, my friend, a journey—your personal healing journey and reunion with God. For all of us, this first step toward healing begins by looking at our childhood experiences. As a growing child, your brain was rapidly developing and establishing patterns that would carry lasting effects throughout your lifetime. Modern science now reveals that the experiences of your childhood affect all future learning, behavior, and even physical health. Neuroscientists, utilizing brain scans, have discovered that there are specific periods of vulnerability tied to specific experiences that include your in-utero life (your life in the womb), birth to age three, and your adolescence. Since you live in a fallen world, you have undoubtedly experienced moments in your formative years that have created subconscious files that are not congruent with the life God offers. These files are certainly not in alignment with the way God sees you. You know, those "tapes" you play over and over again that are not true in the eyes of God. These tapes must transform into truth, and the only way you can truly accomplish this is by opening your heart to God and allowing his divine entry. However, completely opening your heart to God is impossible when you believe wrongly about your worth. Your subconscious mind is likely experiencing a plethora of untruths that are running unchecked, and they need to go.

COMMON SUBCONSCIOUS UN-TRUE TAPES:

- I'm not good enough. (smart enough, pretty enough, etc.)

- Only perfect people are worthy of love.

- I'm unlovable.

- Women can't be trusted.

- Men can't be trusted.

- Rich people are greedy and evil. - Poor people are lazy.

Do any sound familiar? These beliefs, and many like them, limit your ability to reach the fullness God has for you. No one goes through life without struggles. Now this may come as a surprise to you: your belief patterns have the power to propel you forward toward greatness and they also have the power to hold you captive— forever separating you from the greatness God has for you. They can help you become great, reaching your fullest where your God-given gifts benefit you and the world, or they can become the root of self-sabotage, stifling your gifts and killing your dreams of a better life.

> The secret to your ultimate joy lies in the fact that your pain affords you a unique opportunity to reach the oasis of prosperity, happiness, and peace, should you choose to persevere through it.

However, it is the painful beliefs, the untruths that hold the greatest power for real transformation in your life. Yes, you read that correct. Painful beliefs that are not congruent with God's plan for your life hold the greatest power to move you forward into the life God intends for you when you use them correctly! That is what this book is all about. The secret to your ultimate joy lies in the fact that your pain affords you a unique opportunity to reach the oasis of prosperity, happiness, and peace your heart desires - should you choose to persevere through it.

REAL TRANSFORMATION – NOW!

The time for real transformation is now! Mankind is ready, and most importantly, I firmly believe that God is pouring down an abundance of mercy on his children right now to get this done. Can you imagine a world where each and every man, woman, and child is living the fullness of their God-given talents? Can you imagine the innovation that would occur and the relationships that would exist? Can you imagine what your life would look like, your children's lives, your grandchildren's, your parent's lives?

I have been a spiritual seeker for a number of decades, seeking how to find greater prosperity, happiness, and peace in the world. Through it all, I have discovered that the greatest way to find true and lasting happiness is to address the tough times in your life by turning to scripture for guidance. In doing so, I have witnessed a beautiful thread woven throughout sacred scripture—a code of sorts that I call "The Jesus Code." All we have to do is unlock the code. And I'm not just talking about reading scripture as you read the newspaper or your Facebook page. No, I'm talking about a total immersion, where you receive the message and direction within the lines and *between* the lines. God will speak directly to you as he reveals to you his steps for your life. His direction will undoubtedly surprise you many times over.

> I have discovered that the greatest way to find true and lasting happiness is to address the tough times in your life by turning to scripture for guidance.

Through the years I have explored the New Age world, the self-help world, and the Catholic world. I have attended more seminars and workshops, read more books, and listened to more audio recordings than I can begin to imagine. I have prayed. I have meditated. I have been a seeker of truth. I have immersed myself in thousands of Catholic Masses. And I have spent thousands of hours praying in front of the Eucharist. I have found that while each of these drew me closer to Christ, the truths we so desperately need to transform ourselves and the world can best be found inside sacred scripture, inside The Jesus Code. It is all there just waiting to be unlocked.

These truths in scripture demand that we begin by healing our own family, and address the transgenerational entanglements (handed down generational patterns that cause pain) holding us back from reaching our full potential, the patterns passed down from generation to generation. Patterns that negatively impact the development of our children and set the stage for future challenges.

> In order to succeed, we must allow ourselves to surrender to the fact that we are all immersed in the milieu of his son - Jesus Christ.

By supporting such transformation, real change is made today and for the generations to follow. However, for such profound transformation to manifest, it is essential that we realize we are all in this together. There is no separation between God's created beings – his creatures. There is only oneness. Given this, we must participate in God's plan for humanity—together. In order to succeed, we must allow ourselves to surrender to the fact that we are all immersed in the milieu of the most Holy Trinity, God the Father, God the Son, and God the Holy Spirit. From here, God will direct us out of the mess mankind has created.

> Acts 17:28 - "For in him we live and move and have our being; as even some of your own poets have said, 'For we too are his offspring.'"

IMAGINE FOR A MOMENT

Through Christ, all good is possible because it is in him that all of creation came into existence. All over the world, the body of Christ is witnessing real healing and transformation. Yes, hearts and lives are being changed. The ever-evolving field of mental health is ever broadening to include modalities such as biofeedback, eye movement desensitization reprocessing (EMDR), internal family systems (IFS), gestalt therapy, mind-body medicine, healing touch, yoga, and multitudes of self-help books that continually top the best-seller list. This is exciting news, and it reveals our human desire for happiness and

> Through Christ, all good is possible because it is in him that all good exists.

peace. As a community, we are paying greater attention to the emotional and spiritual needs of individuals, and this is cause for hope. However, while we are seeing significant inroads in mankind's approach to healing, I feel there is all too often a missing piece—the piece that needs to be the cornerstone: a full surrender to Jesus Christ—the one who came so that we could have joy within.

Imagine for a moment the tremendous healing humanity would experience if individuals working in the mental health field, the allopathic medical field, the holistic medical field, the coaching field, and the fitness field all surrendered fully to God. Imagine for a moment that they surrendered so fully that they only offered healing modalities that God has revealed to their hearts? What if in addition to yoga, we practiced SoulCore (a core workout that pairs exercise with the Rosary), Pietra Fitness (exercise that features Christian prayer and meditation), or another form of exercise grounded in Jesus' message? Or what if modalities like The LIVE Method (a healing modality that uses acceptance and forgiveness in a Christian setting) and were mainstream? What would the world look like if Contemplative Prayer was widespread and universal? I dare say that multitudes would experience significant, lasting, and miraculous transformation.

> It is God's desire that all of mankind become fully alive.

Even though mankind's collective faith in God has not reached its zenith, God still blesses his children with healing. Miracles still happen each and every day. Amazing, isn't it? I can only assume since you are reading this book that you too desire miracles and transformation in your life. However, I believe that we must bring forth healing modalities that are truly, deeply, and profoundly Christ centered, before we experience the happiness and peace available to us. Modalities created and supported by individuals who choose to become doers of the word—not simply hearers are needed. Contemplatives in action – like the Jesuits. Remember, it is God's desire that all of mankind become fully alive. Many simply need a blueprint to follow, a blueprint grounded in sacred scripture. In this book you will find a road map, a set of monkey bars to hold on to, that will direct you out of the darkness and into the light—into a life where you become whole and healed as your unique gifts are unlocked and released into the world.

> *James 1:22-25 - "But be doers of the word, and not hearers only, deceiving yourselves. For if any one is a hearer of the word and not a doer, he is like a man who observes his natural face in a mirror; for he observes himself and goes away and at once forgets what he was like. But he who looks into the perfect law, the law of liberty, and perseveres, being no hearer that forgets but a doer that acts, he shall be blessed in his doing."*

THE JESUS CODE

In this book, you will find truths in scripture that you may have not known were there—I didn't until I started seeking with deep intent and earnest. Truths that unlock the buried, and not-so-buried, patterns that hold you back from complete happiness and success. You will see how you can beautifully combine scripture with some of

> The freedom divine-like forgiveness offers is beyond comprehension of the human heart and mind, yet it is offered to all of us.

the new advances in the healing world. You will come to understand how transgenerational entanglements lead to physical and emotional disease, trauma, addictions, anxiety, and depression in your life and the lives of your loved ones. You will see how these entanglements hold you back from reaching your full potential. You will see how God has already given you your needed cure in The Jesus Code. You will come to know what it really means to carry your cross—it is probably not what you think.

The power of forgiveness will be released, and your heart will transform. Can you imagine a life where forgiveness is easy and you experience only love and acceptance for those around you? That person who drives you crazy, imagine your heart filled with forgiveness and love for them. Wouldn't that feel so much better! What peace your heart will experience when this happens with all who enter into your life. However, this will not be your "forgive and forget" drive-through variety of forgiveness. You will experience giving divine-like forgiveness. The freedom divine-like forgiveness offers is beyond the comprehension of the human heart and mind, yet it is offered to all of us.

> We are created in the image of God and given this we can offer forgiveness that resembles his forgiveness, we can offer divine-like forgiveness.

Divine forgiveness is different. It does not leave the victim full of guilt, anger, longing, or resentment if he or she is unable to forgive. No, divine forgiveness is the forgiveness that Christ offered as he was nailed to the cross, the forgiveness he has for each and every one of us. The forgiveness that truly sets our hearts free. We are created in the image of God, and given this, we can offer forgiveness that resembles his forgiveness, we can offer divine-like forgiveness.

Luke 23:34 - Jesus said, "Father, forgive them; for they do not know what they are doing." And they cast lots to divide his clothing.

You see, God, the creator of the entire universe, has revealed all we need for our transformation in sacred scripture – a golden thread of sorts. The Jesus Code is the golden thread I have witnessed throughout scripture. His words are true, his words are eternal, and you can trust in his words as you tackle the darkness in your body, heart, and mind. Once tackled, your family and the generations to follow will surely live.

HOW TO SEE AND ABSORB THE JESUS CODE

You will see The Jesus Code woven through this entire book, it is uniquely presented so your heart can receive profound healing, just like mine did when I first saw the code. The Jesus Code is found in the stories, in The Nine Faces of Struggle, in the commentary, in the meditations, and in the scripture offered. It is found in the lines and in-between the lines. It is not a simple formula, yet it can be easily received. Much like the beautiful sound of an orchestra is an experience beyond sheets of music, instruments and musicians, and an exquisite oil painting is more then it's canvas and paint; The Jesus Code lives beyond the words presented in this book. I recommend reading this book cover to cover so that you can absorb The Jesus Code fully. Please read each scripture passage carefully, giving yourself time to reflect on each one in light of what is written. Please do not read ahead to a chapter that catches your heart. You will be presented important foundation components to The Jesus Code in each chapter, beginning here with the Introduction. These components are important for you to integrate prior to reading further. It is my greatest desire that each chapter touches your heart and builds upon your prior reading in such a way that you see the world differently so that your relationship with God changes in such a way that miracles happen spontaneously in your life.

THE JESUS CODE CONNECTION

The Jesus Code Connection is offered to help you receive and understand The Jesus Code more fully. You are invited to allow its words "sit" with you for a time – in silent contemplation after you have read each section. Take your time and enjoy the journey. The Jesus Code Connection is woven throughout this book in an attempt to help your heart open to the truth your creator has for you. A word, or two or three, is offered for your reflection as you meditate a bit on what you just read.

All of this is presented in such a way as to help you develop a deep and more loving relationship with your creator, a relationship where you receive all you need to live a life fully alive. The Jesus Code is beautifully intricate, while holding a soft simplicity and The Jesus Code Connection will assist you on your journey.

Consider this book a gift on your spiritual quest for truth, happiness and peace. Mark it up, annotate, highlight the lines that speak to you; doodle on its pages if you feel called, and make it your own. In the end I hope I have been of service to you, to your heart and to your soul.

> *John 6:5 - "I am the living bread which came down from heaven; if any one eats of this bread, he will live forever; and the bread which I shall give for the life of the world is my flesh."*

> *Jeremiah 31:33 - "But this is the covenant which I will make with the house of Israel after those days, says the Lord: I will put my law within them, and I will write it upon their hearts; and I will be their God, and they shall be my people."*

THE JESUS CODE CONNECTION
Reflect - Transform - Enjoy

« Chapter 1 »

Complexities of the Modern Person

A NOTE FROM THE AUTHOR

If you have not already read the Introduction, I kindly ask that you start there. You see, The Jesus Code is sprinkled throughout this entire book in a harmonized rhythm—beginning with the Introduction. This code provides an opportunity to unlock the blocks interfering with you living your life to the fullest. The Introduction is short, however, very foundational, and besides, it will make me happy if you read it first because I gave it considerable thought before I penned its words! Many thanks and God bless— Carolyn.

A PEOPLE OF HOPE

It appears that mankind is more aware of its need for happiness and peace than ever before. This is a wonderful thing! A shift has most certainly begun. We have programs and projects all directed toward bettering humanity and supporting those who are less privileged. We witness missionaries traveling to third-world countries, tending to the needs of the vulnerable, sick, and impoverished. Caring individuals engage in fundraisers for various causes to support our brothers and sisters suffering from physical and emotional pains.

Today's emphasis toward a greater understanding of mental and emotional health and the support offered to suffering individuals is unparalleled. We have even dubbed May as Mental Health Awareness month. In the last couple of decades alone, we have witnessed sweeping changes in the mental health fields of psychology, psychiatry, and social work. The healing arts of massage, acupuncture, and more modalities such as yoga and mindfulness are becoming part of our daily vernacular. They have become infused into the fabric of our everyday lives. The quickly emerging field of self-help gurus, life coaches, and empowerment professionals is leaving a healing imprint on society as well. All of this is a breath of fresh air and a sign that the fabric of humanity is rapidly changing. We are a people looking for more, we seek healing, we seek greater happiness, and we are becoming extremely desiring of peace. Yes, this shift will certainly serve to facilitate the healing of broken hearts and broken families. We are becoming free, and our God-given gifts are being released into the world. However, we are at a critical point in humanity and our transformation is far from complete.

> Isaiah 65:17 - "For I am about to create new
> heavens and a new earth; the former things shall
> not be remembered or come to mind."

While there is much good going on in the world, there is also significant pain and heartache. When we look around, we do not see what one might expect, given the vast goodness expressed in the world. People still experience unfulfilled dreams, families are still broken, and individuals are still isolated with a sense of loneliness. Horrific crimes are still being committed against the most vulnerable of society and the most vulnerable in our very own families. Individuals walk around with hate in their hearts, unforgiveness acts as a brutal shield, and many more walk around holding unfulfilled dreams within.

What are we missing? Why are we still seeing brokenness handed down generation after generation?

Not long ago I volunteered at the Indianapolis Women's Prison, a position I held for over two years. During my time I witnessed significant human pain. I witnessed generations of incarcerated women beginning with grandmother, mother, and then granddaughter—it was heartbreaking. In like fashion, mankind still witnesses generations of poverty, mental illness, child abuse, trauma, and addictions. Given that we are all one body in Christ, this must change.

We already have within our minds and hearts the dreams that have the power to break these cycles and allow us to enter into a world where only goodness abounds. Maybe we are not asking the right questions. Perhaps instead of asking what is wrong with people, maybe the better question becomes one of where to search for the solution.

Where should we look for insight and true guidance? Where should we invest our precious resources of time, talent, and treasure? Should we turn to our governments? After all, many of today's governments, especially the first-world governments, have programs set in place to serve the most vulnerable of society. Should we turn to community programs that seek to better the world through altruism? Should we turn to our churches? I believe that in order to unearth the real solution, we must first make a conscious decision as to where we are going to invest ourselves. Are we going to invest our personal resources in the things of this earth? Or are we going to give of ourselves to the things that are God's? We have free will to choose, yet if we desire to fully live, we must choose the path of life.

> Matthew 22:21 - They answered, "The emperor's."
> Then he said to them, "Give therefore to the
> emperor the things that are the emperor's, and to
> God the things that are God's."

THE JESUS CODE CONNECTION
Hope – New Life

IN SEARCH OF LOVE

Consider for a moment a young child who desires to master a new skill such as riding a bike or jumping rope. The child wants to acquire this ability more than anything because he or she believes that once mastered, this new activity will surely promise to bring forth greater happiness and love in her life. So the child, singularly focused, begins the process of mastery while holding in her heart the end goal. The child invests the resources of time and perseverance necessary for mastery, and eventually, mastery is accomplished. The new skill is obtained, and the real goal of enjoying life in a new way with others is possible. The next time the invitation to jump rope with friends is extended, the child's heart is filled with excitement and hope. Now the family bike ride is filled with a sense of accomplishment and pride. It was the singular focus that enabled the child to accomplish her goal of mastery and the ultimate goal of happiness the newly acquired skill set promised.

As beautiful as this story of accomplishment is, the joy the little child experienced is not yet complete. More happiness and peace await her in her lifetime. If she were to stop seeking greater fulfillment once she mastered these two new skills, her happiness and peace would eventually give way to despair and pain. No human being would feel complete having only mastered bike riding and rope skipping in their life. Human beings, by our very nature, continually seek and yearn for more. Given this, it is important to direct our seeking toward the path that promises the fulfillment of our ever-seeking nature. The happiness and peace we seek can only be found in the infinite goodness of God.

> *Luke 11:9 - "And I tell you, ask, and it will be given you; seek, and you will find; knock, and it will be opened to you."*

Looking around at the world, we can suppose that we are now aware that mankind, like the rope-skipping and bike-riding little child, wants more out of life. We want to ride the bike and we want to skip rope! We are in the ball game and we have the equipment necessary. The goal of happiness is in sight and we believe it is attainable. However, I would argue that we have not yet properly set our intentions and, therefore, we have not fully directed our time, talent, and treasures in a way that serves us to best reach our goal of happiness and peace. We need to refine our search and narrow our parameters.

Perhaps you too have been searching, trying to learn how to ride the bike and skip rope. Undoubtedly, you have had many false starts in life. However, with each false start, like Thomas Edison, you are presented with an opportunity to learn a valuable lesson.

> *Thomas Edison - I have not failed. I've just found 10,000 ways that won't work.*

Fortunately, for me, I did find a way to happiness, prosperity, and inner peace. After years of trials, tribulations, false starts, half starts, and painful experiences, perseverance won out. While I will not say I have arrived, I boldly proclaim that I have discovered the real way to a life of happiness, peace, and fulfillment. Perhaps like my life, yours is paved with cobblestones of self-discovery, wound healing, family awareness, forgiveness, acceptance, and most of all, surrendering to a power much bigger than myself. Yes, a power beyond all comprehension that gently guides and directs my every step on the path toward wholeness is where I place all my trust.

This power has already prepared for you the place of true, lasting abundance, happiness, and peace should you choose to live there as well. This power has already

> You already know how to ride the bike, you already know how to jump rope. You only need to access the roadmap that is already imprinted in your heart.

promised you full union with the source of all life and goodness. This power holds you close to his sacred heart, whether you know it or not. This power lives in your heart and guarantees that you already know the way to happiness and peace—you already know how to ride the bike, you already know how to jump rope. You only need to access the road map that is already imprinted in your heart.

> *1 Corinthians 3:16 - Do you not know that you are God's temple and that God's Spirit dwells in you?*

THE JESUS CODE CONNECTION
Dream – Trust

HOW TO SEEK AND FIND

You see, Jesus Christ has already told you everything you need to know: he is the way, the truth, and the life. He has promised you that God has sent his Holy Spirit to abide within and all around your heart. You live in the healing milieu of the Holy Spirit – the milieu of love itself. The only catch is that you must love him and remain in his love. When you see Jesus, you see the creator of all, the One who is the Alpha and the Omega—the One who has the power to draw you into everlasting happiness.

Christ is your road map to happiness and peace. He has but one request: he asks that you choose to follow him and put aside your worldly desires. While putting aside your worldly desires may sound scary, it is not a difficult or impossible task to accomplish. The Jesus Code will reveal to you how easy it can be to follow Jesus and receive happiness and peace beyond your wildest imagination.

> *John 14: 6-7 - "I am the way, and the truth, and the life. No one comes to the Father except through me. If you know me, you will know my Father also. From now on you do know him and have seen him."*

Jesus has told you that to fix your eyes on him is to fix your eyes upon the Father—the source of all life. Jesus Christ is the bridge between heaven and earth, between pain and healing. All life came into existence through Him. Through him, his followers are promised entry into heavenly bliss. However, you must first allow the source of all life to draw you up from the murkiness of this world into the serenity of eternal life. This is the aspiration of this book— that you find the path that your heart yearns for. You can walk out of the pain, the hurt, the heartache and run into your dreams of abundance, happiness, and peace when you travel within the milieu of the Holy Trinity.

> *John 14:16-17 - "And I will ask the Father, and he will give you another Advocate, to be with you forever. This is the Spirit of truth, whom the world cannot receive, because it neither sees him nor knows him. You know him, because he abides with you, and he will be in you."*

Living a life of your dreams is available to each and every human being walking the face of this earth. As you read this book, you will dive into the many questions regarding salvation and just who Jesus was referring to when he said, "No one comes to the Father except through me"—the findings may surprise you. This was a statement of inclusion, not exclusion. However, for now, it is important to realize that real hope does exist and you can live a life of fullness and happiness.

> Living a life of your dreams is available to each and every human being walking the face of this earth.

> *Revelation 21:4 - "He will wipe every tear from their eyes. Death will be no more; mourning and crying and pain will be no more, for the first things have passed away."*

TOGETHER WE CAN CHANGE THE WORLD

Unfortunately, many will never find a way to facilitate the healing of the broken cobblestones in their lives and the lives of their loved ones. Too many people will continue to suffer needlessly. Toxic patterns will repeat, passing into future generations. Transgenerational entanglements will continue. People will continue to live a life of unrealized dreams, under the dark clouds of heartache, unforgiveness, and despair. The sheep will remain lost, yet the Shepard will continue to seek and find them.

> *Psalm 107: 19-20 - Then they cried out to the LORD in their trouble, and he saved them out of their distresses. He sent his word and healed them, and delivered them from their destructions.*

You can make a difference—we can make a difference. By addressing the patterns within your family that run counter to God's desire for mankind you will find freedom. New life is available to the world, and the shift has already begun. I have seen it and I sit in awe. Many have moved into a new life already. For me personally, I understand what it means to transition from a life of heartache and pain into a life of fullness and abundance by addressing the transgenerational entanglements of my own family. I have moved beyond the introverted, dissociated little child from a broken home; I have moved beyond the pregnant, impoverished eighteen-year-old single mother with a tenth grade education; I have moved beyond the unconscious wife and mother; I have moved beyond the frustrated business woman; and I have been transformed into the happy, fulfilled successful fifty-five-year-old wife, mother, and grandmother behind the pen today. Is my life perfect today? No, there are still raw, open wounds in my heart that God is healing. But now my trust and faith in His plan for my life far supersedes my pain. I have found true freedom. The rest of the world's suffering people can also experience this type of freedom.

> *Psalm 118:5 - Out of my distress I called on the Lord; the Lord answered me and set me free.*

Yes, there will be many bumps and bruises along the way; however, once these injuries have been transformed into the precious jewels of hope, forgiveness, understanding, acceptance, and love, freedom and abundance are the end result. I can assure you that more goodness is on the way for you, your family, and the world. We all have our stories of brokenheartedness and pain, we all have our bumps and bruises. So let's transform them together into precious, divine jewels. Yes, we have work to do and the world needs true transformation. So let's do this thing!

THE JESUS CODE CONNECTION
Desire More

« Chapter 2 »

Thoughts Are Powerful Things

Ignatius of Loyola - "Act as if everything depended on you; trust as if everything depended on God."

C onsider for a moment a little child who has just picked wild flowers to give to her mother. While picking the flowers, she was filled with love for her mommy, she anticipated the moment when she would offer this exquisite heartfelt gift to her mother. She anticipated the smile on her mother's face, the embrace her mother would offer, and the sense of internal warmth of the moment. Perhaps she even thought of the vase her mother would place her gift in, visual evidence of the love the two of them share together, for the entire family to see. The little child was immersed in the thought and anticipation of mommy love.

However, as is the nature of the world we live in, much more was going on around her. While the little girl (or boy) was focused on her mother's love, she was also surrounded by much more than she was able to take in. The beauty of the sunshine, the cool green grass under her feet, the gentle warmth of the summer breeze, and the summer fragrance of the air were all around her, yet she almost certainly took little notice of them. Significant beauty surrounded her, yet her singularly focused heart didn't perceive it.

> When we remember and honor that it is through Christ all of the earth exists we begin to understand that it is only through him, and him alone, we will find happiness and peace.

As a young child, this little girl was free to be expressly focused on her love for her mother while others were providing all of the experiences surrounding the moment. Her father was perhaps at work providing for the family. Out of his labors came the provisions that purchased the groceries for her morning breakfast and her other worldly needs. Perhaps it was he who planted the grass seed, fertilized the land, or bought the vase for her mom. Her mother was also quietly offering comfort and nurture. Perhaps she made her daughter's breakfast and helped her with her hair that morning, perhaps she laundered her clothes and gave her the morning hug and kiss that beckoned the gathering of a bouquet of flowers.

And behind it all, we have the creator of the universe setting into motion all that it took for the grass to grow, the flowers to bloom, and for the child to live, breathe, and walk the earth. There is always much more than what comes to the forefront of our conscious mind, regardless of where we are on our spiritual journey. When we remember and honor that it is through Christ all of the earth exists, we begin to understand that it is only through him, and him alone, that we will find happiness and peace.

> *Colossians 1:15-16 - He is the image of the invisible God, the firstborn of all creation; for in him all things in heaven and on earth were created, things visible and invisible, whether thrones or dominions or rulers or powers—all things have been created through him and for him.*

MISSING THE FOREST FROM THE TREES

Much like the little girl, we tend to see the small details, sometimes with great love and emotion as she experienced in the gathering of flowers. However, like the little child, we don't and can't absorb all that surrounds us. It takes maturity, faith, and continued heartfelt prayer to appreciate the fullness of the divine milieu of which we are immersed within—Christ himself. Just as the little girl could not comprehend the totality of her experience as she picked those

> The human person is very small, and yet simultaneously wholly cared for and loved beyond measure by a loving creator.

flowers, as a human being you can never fully comprehend what your creator has set in motion for you. You are continually being offered a glimpse into the truth. This glimpse is offered in perfect order for your soul's healing and growth. To more fully peer behind the sacred veil and receive God's word, you must go to where his word lives. You must immerse yourself in sacred scripture with reverence, fervency, and surrender in order to receive his word.

I invite you to continue to cultivate what has been set into motion within you as you read this book; breathe in the beauty of the flowers and stay present with them. Eventually, you will be called to be mindful of the grass under your feet and the warmth of the sunshine. There is no end to the expansion that awaits you as you journey toward greater happiness and peace. God is infinite. The key is learning how to surrender and allow yourself to be guided

> To more fully peer behind the sacred veil and receive God's word you must go to where his word lives, and you must immerse yourself in sacred scripture with reverence, fervency and surrender in order to receive his word.

through the truth. Of all the things I have learned on my spiritual quest, it is that there is one basic truth that holds steadfast: The human person is very small and yet simultaneously wholly cared for and loved beyond measure by a loving, infinite creator. Let me repeat that again. Take a moment and read this line one more time: The human person is very small and yet simultaneously wholly cared for and loved beyond measure by a loving, infinite creator. Our God gently holds the fabric of the world together. Within him alone will we find the happiness and peace we seek. When we surrender and focus on love, like the child gathering flowers, and allow him to care for us he will lead us to a place where our dreams are manifested.

> *Matthew 19:14 - But Jesus said, "Let the little children come to me, and do not stop them; for it is too such as these that the kingdom of heaven belongs."*

THE JESUS CODE CONNECTION
Pure Love

SOWING SEEDS

I must confess something. I did not start my spiritual quest in a place of childlike surrender. Who does? Perhaps like you, I needed to know; I needed to have some sense of control over my destiny. If I could garner enough knowledge about the heavens, the natural world, and its various healing modalities, then I would experience the happiness and peace I longed for—and that I longed to bring forth into the world. People were hurting, myself included, and my heart deeply desired to find the cure. Perhaps this sounds familiar.

We live in a complex world where all seekers will find themselves in the proverbial candy store; the trick is to find the Golden Ticket. Once my journey began, I couldn't get enough. My seeking led to my attendance of more nutritional, herbal, homeopathic, and holistic medicine seminars than I can even begin to remember. During each, I met amazing healing practitioners of all kinds. I enjoyed the company of other naturopathic doctors, medical doctors, chiropractic doctors, Chinese medicine doctors, acupuncturists, massage therapists, and energy healers of all kinds. We engaged in deep conversations that ranged from natural medicine to energy healing to various world philosophies and religions. Through it all, I observed a common thread woven through our conversations. Inside each of us lives a heartfelt desire for happiness and peace, a desire we wish to bring forth into the world.

I believe that every human being holds the same desire deep within, a desire to do well and be of service to one another. However, for many reasons, this desire may need to be rekindled if it has been smoldering for a while, or extinguished altogether. We can start doing this by being mindful of our thoughts and emotions. Your thoughts and emotions arise from somewhere. Try for a moment to stop thinking. You can't do it, can you? It is estimated that the average person has anywhere from 50,000–70,000 thoughts a day. Wow—that's a big number.

While you may have had a hand in the creation of a significant number of your thoughts, a good majority of them are spontaneous, coming from somewhere outside of you. Like a flame, it requires a spark. Your thoughts have an original seed and impetus that ignited them. In order to live a happy, peaceful life, we must nurture and care for the seeds of God. When we care for and nurture his seeds, all the others will fall away in due time.

> *Matthew 13:24-29 - "The kingdom of heaven is like a farmer who planted good seed in his field. But that night as the workers slept, his enemy came and planted weeds among the wheat, then slipped away. When the crop began to grow and produce grain, the weeds also grew. The farmer's workers went to him and said, 'Sir, the field where you planted that good seed is full of weeds! Where did they come from?' 'An enemy has done this!' the farmer exclaimed. 'Should we pull out the weeds?'*

they asked. 'No,' he replied, 'you'll uproot the wheat
if you do. Let both grow together until the harvest.
Then I will tell the harvesters to sort out the weeds,
tie them into bundles, and burn them, and to put
the wheat in the barn.'"

When you give greater attention to thoughts that are congruent with God's plan for your life, you will begin to have more thoughts that nourish the good seed within you. However, can you always have thoughts of goodness, is this even possible? We can take a que from those happy-go-lucky people in the world. They tend to have an abundance of happy-go-lucky thoughts on a regular basis. The difference between them and the doomsday folks is that they have made a decision to focus on the positive, to be mindful of thoughts of goodness and thoughts supportive of their dreams. Since your behavior follows your thoughts, when you enjoy thoughts of goodness, you cultivate the seeds of God. Of course, this is not to say you will never have another negative thought once you have reached happiness, because, after all, harmful thoughts that lead to the development of weeds arise from time to time. The question then becomes, what are you going to do about the thoughts that are not congruent with your dreams?

> When you give greater attention to thoughts that are congruent with God's plan for your life, you will begin to have more thoughts that nourish the good seed within you.

Proverbs 17:22 - King Solomon suggested that "a
merry heart doeth good like a medicine."

REPROGRAMMING TIPS

Modern science has revealed that there exists a window of time when your subconscious mind is highly susceptible to suggestion.

Since your subconscious mind is the part of your mind that controls about 95 percent of your behavior, this is a big deal. Yet many individuals fill this period of time with doomsday information that will cause them to fret and worry even when there is nothing to fret or worry about.

So when is this magical moment? Well, it's the last ten minutes before you fall asleep. Whatever information you exposed yourself to during this time, your subconscious mind will continue to process it for the next four to five hours. So let's use this time to your fullest benefit! Here are a few recommendations I offer my clients:

- Read and meditate on scripture before bed.

- Read uplifting books before sleep, stories of human triumph.

- Read books on the Catholic saints and other church leaders.

- Pray a Rosary or a Chaplet of Divine Mercy—make sure you offer it up with an uplifting intention. If you fall asleep during prayer, simply pick up the next day or in the morning where you left off or ask your guardian angel to finish it for you.

- Practice Lectio Divina. This is a form of meditation over Sacred Scripture. To learn more about this type of prayer I invite you to visit my website TheLIVEMethod.com.

- If you must watch TV (which I generally advise against), make sure it is uplifting programming.

- Avoid watching the news and other late-night shows (before bed or any other time) like the plague. Few people are mentally and spiritually strong enough to handle such media. If you really need to know something, someone will tell you about it.

- Create a healthy sleep routine so when you slip into bed, it feels like an escape from the world.

- Using essential oils and restful sounds can be very helpful.

- Do not eat or work on your computer while in bed. Reserve your bed for sleeping.

- Ask the Holy Spirit to guide your thoughts during sleep.

  Romans 12:2 - Do not be conformed to this world, but be transformed by the renewing of your minds, so that you may discern what is the will of God— what is good and acceptable and perfect.

> ### THE JESUS CODE CONNECTION
> *Jesus Centered Mindfulness*

« Chapter 3 »

How to Live Fully Alive

2 Corinthians 8:2- For in a severe test of affliction, their abundance of joy and their extreme poverty have overflowed in a wealth of liberality on their part.

I f you are like most of mankind, you are probably not living the life of your dreams. More than likely, you squander some of your precious energy chasing wants and desires that delude you with false promises. Material possessions, praise, prestige, power, and worldly influence have taunted many a person since Adam and Eve ate of the forbidden fruit. When such worldly preoccupations interfere with God's plan for your life, heartache and pain will follow—just like the pain our first parents experienced once they believed the lies of the serpent.

Genesis 3:4-5 - But the serpent said to the woman, "You will not die. For God knows that when you eat of it your eyes will be opened, and you will be like God, knowing good and evil."

Remember, once Adam and Eve ate of the forbidden fruit, everything changed in their lives. When they heard God in the garden, instead of running to him with childlike excitement, they hid and covered themselves. Why did they hide? Why did they cover themselves? They hid from God because they were afraid and filled with shame.

> *Genesis 3:9-10 - But the Lord God called to the man, and said to him, "Where are you?" And he said, "I heard the sound of thee in the garden, and I was afraid, because I was naked; and I hid myself.*

Fear is powerful, and it can rip us away from our benevolent creator if we allow it to do so. Fear is a tool the Evil One uses against us— the liar who came to steal, kill, and destroy, the one who is in the world. Fear and shame are the first two means he used to separate mankind from God—no wonder they hold so much power in our lives.

Yet we must always remember that Satan is powerless at the hands of God; God the Father, Son, and Holy Spirit. Jesus, the one who dwells within us, has the power to overcome all evil in the world.

> *1 John 4:4 - Little children, you are of God, and have overcome them; for he who is in you is greater than he who is in the world.*

> *John 14:27 - "Peace I leave with you; my peace I give to you. I do not give to you as the world gives. Do not let your hearts be troubled, and do not let them be afraid."*

More on the Evil One and how to break his hold in your life, the lives of your loved ones, and in the world in upcoming chapters.

THE JESUS CODE CONNECTION
Deceived – Victorious

REFORMATTING THE SUBCONSCIOUS MIND

Your subconscious mind holds tremendous influence over your everyday behavior and desires. Remember, about 95 percent of your behavior is controlled by your subconscious mind. So if your mother found happiness in a chocolate chip cookie then you will likely seek to find it there as well. Your files most likely deceive you over and over again, and most of these have been passed down to you from the generations that came before. Happiness and true peace will come when you surrender, when you allow your subconscious files to be rewritten with the truth. To be fully happy, you need to claim the power of your subconscious mind and align it with the mind of God—it needs divine reformatting. You do not need to spend your days treading down dead-end roads, and most of all, you do not need to give up hope for a better world altogether. By rewriting your subconscious files with the truth, you become free to live the life of your dreams. Once rewritten, it will become clear which path to take in your life and which path will lead to your perfection as a child of God.

> Happiness and true peace will come when you surrender, when you allow your subconscious files to be rewritten with the truth.

James 4:7 - Submit yourselves therefore to God.
Resist the devil and he will flee from you.

God has already given you everything you need for happiness and peace, yet you may not be copiously familiar with the words in sacred scripture. I'm still working on that one myself. Once you begin to develop insight into sacred scripture, everything will begin to open up to you. Using The Jesus Code, you will find the power to transform your life. The process begins when you choose to follow him.

THE JESUS CODE CONNECTION
New Life

THE UNHOLY ATTACK

Unfortunately, all too often our modern church does little to meet individuals at their deepest wounds. I certainly don't blame our churches. After all, if you were the Evil One and you wanted to block God's healing, wouldn't your first logical move be aimed at gaining entry into the hearts and minds of the children in God's church? Wouldn't you want them to judge one another, exclude one another, and hurt one another? Wouldn't you want to do everything possible to hide the truth from them—knowing full well that the truth is found there under their rooftops?

Let's look at the attack on the early church. Early Christians were brutally martyred and killed for their faith. Yet, this did not stop the spread of Christianity. The next attack was directed at the internal working of the church—at the hearts and minds of its members. Division followed, and we now have more than 33,000 different forms of Christianity in the world.

Far too many people today are afraid to enter their church and lay bare their inner pain. They fear exclusion or abandonment from their fellow church members will follow. Generally speaking, we don't speak about the deep wounds in humanity in our places of worship as much as we could. Further, we don't invite in the most wounded among us as much as Jesus would like for us to do. This needs to change. Fortunately, we don't need to look far for guidance and support.

HOW TO COUNTER SUCH AN ATTACK

Our early church fathers meditated extensively on sacred scripture, and in doing so, they developed a deep understanding of the transformational power held within its words. Arguably, their passion for sacred scripture stands as the foundation of Christianity. A powerful force entered into our planet after the physical death of Jesus Christ, a force that facilitated the expansion of the greatest and longest standing movement the world has ever seen: Christianity. Looking back, we lay witness to the undeniable role sacred scripture and the teachings of the early church fathers held in the spread of Christianity. Today the world needs a new birth; the world needs to chart another course, a course that has the power to transform all of humanity. I have come to believe that this can be accomplished when we return to what has been proven to work: an increased meditation on sacred scripture.

> *Colossians 3:15-17 - And let the peace of Christ rule in your hearts, to which indeed you were called in the one body. And be thankful. Let the word of Christ dwell in you richly, as you teach and admonish one another in all wisdom, and as you sing psalms and hymns and spiritual songs with thankfulness in your hearts to God. And whatever you do, in word or deed, do everything in the name of the Lord Jesus, giving thanks to God the Father through him.*

THE JESUS CODE CONNECTION
Battle – Divine Victory

THE RULER OF THIS WORLD

Before you can accurately walk your path into abundance, happiness, and peace, you must first develop an understanding of the powers in the world and who indeed rules this world we live in: Satan. Indeed, the world is riddled with unfulfilled dreams, and this makes perfect sense for one reason: the ruler of this world is a liar who has come to steal, kill, and destroy. He seeks to steal your hope and your dreams, he seeks to kill the love in your heart for your brothers and sisters, and he seeks to destroy all of mankind so that each and every one of us does not enter into the fullness of our glory. He uses his lies to accomplish this. He will manipulate, he will lie, he will prey on your weakness, your fear and even your love in an attempt to draw you away from the happiness and peace God has for you.

> *John 14:30-31 - "I will no longer talk much with you, for the ruler of this world is coming. He has no power over me; but I do as the Father has commanded me, so that the world may know that I love the Father. Rise, let us go hence."*
> *- Jesus Christ to his disciples prior to his crucifixion.*

Wherever God has placed his seed of divinity in this world, Satan desires to utilize whatever means possible to prevent it from yielding new life. Yet Satan can only do his work when you accept his lies as truth and act upon them. This is accomplished through sin. When you accept his lies and take action based on this information, you participate in his evil works. His sinful kingdom then expands. The result is the loss of the fullness of life that leads to your happiness and peace. Sometimes your inclination to sin is the result of generational pain passed down to you. However, always remember that God never stops seeking his lost children. It's time to put an end to the Evil One's claim on you and your family. Remember, you are promised a new life in Christ.

> *John 10:10 - "The thief comes only to steal and kill and destroy; I have come that they may have life, and have it to the full."*

When you participate with Satan in propagating his wretched agenda, it is done through sin and at the hands of the gift of free will, which God has given you. Sadly, this is often done without your knowledge or awareness—remember, Satan is the great deceiver. Satan is not a creator. He can only "rule" over what has already been created. Satan, in his angel wisdom (albeit fallen), knows that in order to rule over you, he must first gain entry. This entry point is sin. He presents himself as beautiful, enticing, and desirous. Remember, he was the angel of light before he turned his back on God. He knows how to perfectly disguise himself so he can tempt you away from God. Through the violation of God's law, Satan—in his jealousy, envy, pride, and anger—obtains entry into God's most precious creation: you and all of mankind.

Yes, all angels, fallen and God's angels alike, possess a wisdom beyond human wisdom. Angels can see the spiritual world in ways humanity cannot. However, God's angels, out of humility and love for God, desire to protect, guide, and minister to you. Whereas the fallen angels, out of their jealousy over God's love for you, seek to lead you into sin and away from the happiness and peace God promises you. It is through the human nature of Jesus Christ that you will also find yourself to be more precious than angels in the eyes of God.

> *Hebrews 1:4-6 - (Jesus) having become as much superior to angels as the name he has obtained is more excellent than theirs. For to what angel did God ever say, "Thou art my Son, today I have begotten thee"? Or again, "I will be to him a father, and he shall be to me a son"? And again, when he brings the first-born into the world, he says, "Let all God's angels worship him."*

THE JESUS CODE CONNECTION
Sin – Angels – Truth

SATAN IS A LIAR

Always remember who is at the source of the pain humanity experiences. The liar who seeks to destroy and separate you from God.

- He will cause you to be filled with shame so you hide from God.

- He will make you afraid to approach God.

- He will cause you to go blind, unable to see the truth of who you truly are.

- He will cause to you feel unworthy and not good enough.

- He will isolate you from others in an attempt to have your ear all to himself.

- His evil works will blind you from fully receiving the word of God if you don't stop him.

- He will convince you that you don't need God or his church.

- He will cause you to hide your goodness from the world.

It's all a lie. You are good enough, you are worthy of love, and you need to unite with a community of believers where you can carry and heal your burdens together. This is all true for one simple reason: you are created in the image of a communal God and you are his child. However, you must realize the truth about this world you live in and what the agenda of its ruler is. Once you grasp these truths, you can begin to see where you have been blinded and where you need to turn to find the abundance and happiness your heart desires.

> *2 Corinthians 4:4 - Satan, who is the god of this evil world, has made him blind, unable to see the glorious light of the Gospel that is shining upon him or to understand the amazing message we preach about the glory of Christ, who is God.*

God does not offer suboptimal change through healing. No, he offers real healing and transformation – real food for your soul that will awaken it to a full life.

When you use your free will to surrender to God the seed of divinity he has placed within your heart begins to take root. If nourished properly it will produce divine fruit in perfect time. However, due to the pain you have experienced at the hands of sin in this world the healing and cultivating required must be allowed the time necessary for holy germination. God does not offer suboptimal change through healing. No, he offers real healing and transformation—real food for your soul that will awaken it to a full life.

> *Ecclesiastes 3:1-2 - For everything there is a*
> *season, and a time for every matter under heaven:*
> *a time to be born, and a time to die; a time to plant,*
> *and a time to pluck up what is planted.*

Yet, when we seek healing, when we seek truth, and when we seek God we live a life of freedom – a life that is only available to God's children.

The time to pluck is now. That burning desire in your heart to be happy is real and possible. As I mentioned earlier, the world is at a beautiful place. God is pouring down blessings upon those who seek to join him in this new world, and it is time for you to claim your blessings!

In choosing to follow Christ, you are assured freedom from pain and freedom from transgenerational entanglements. It is not only possible, but it is also the will of God. Yet you must choose to surrender, and this can be done by looking at your troubles and following God's plan for healing. This choice to follow Christ will undoubtedly be filled with challenges and setbacks because we live in a fallen world, among fallen people. Yet, when we seek healing, when we seek truth, and when we seek God, we live a life of freedom—a life that is only available to God's children.

*1 John 5:19 - We know that we are children of God
and that all the rest of the world around us is
under Satan's power and control.*

THE JESUS CODE CONNECTION
Prince of Lies – Limited – Free Will

CAN WE REALLY DO GREATER WORKS THAN JESUS?

*John 14:12 - "Amen, amen, I say to you, whoever
believes in me will do the works that I do, and will
do greater ones than these, because I am going to
the Father."*

Amazing, Jesus Christ told us that we not only can do greater works
than he did, he told us that we indeed *will* do greater works when
we believe in him. How can this be? After all, Jesus Christ is God
incarnate, fully man and fully God. How can we even come close to
doing the great works our Savior accomplished when he walked the
earth? Before we dive into the how, we must first examine a bit of
the healing Jesus performed during his earthly ministry.

Sacred scripture is rich with stories
of the instantaneous physical
healing Jesus brought to those who
sought him. We read of Jesus
healing lepers, sons, daughters,
brothers, demonic possessed
individuals, women, men,
distressed individuals—multitudes
upon multitudes of people were
healed at the hands of Jesus Christ.
God's children were drawn to him
and the masses flocked to him in

> Sacred scripture is rich
> with stories of the
> instantaneous physical
> healing Jesus brought to
> those who sought him.

search of healing. The world really hasn't changed that much has it? We are still hurting, and we still seek the healing of a savior. Yet imagine for a moment what the world would look like if each and every one of us believed in the Jesus of John 14:12, if each and every one of us did such great works of healing?

> *Mark 10:52 - "Go," said Jesus, "your faith has healed you." Immediately he received his sight and followed Jesus along the road.*
>
> *Matthew 8:3 - Jesus reached out his hand and touched the man. "I am willing," he said. "Be clean!" Immediately he was cleansed of his leprosy.*
>
> *Matthew 9:22 - Jesus turned and saw her. "Take heart, daughter," he said, "your faith has healed you." And the woman was healed at that moment.*
>
> *Mark 5:29 - Immediately her bleeding stopped and she felt in her body that she was freed from her suffering.*
>
> *Mark 3:10 - For he had healed many, so that those with diseases were pushing forward to touch him.*
>
> *Matt 8:16-17- When evening had come, they brought to Him many who were demon-possessed. And He cast out the spirits with a word, and healed all who were sick, that it might be fulfilled which was spoken by Isaiah the prophet, saying: "He Himself took our infirmities and bore our sicknesses."*

THE JESUS CODE CONNECTION
Faith – Power - Healing

Jesus, who was filled with such magnificent power, walked the earth healing all those who believed in him - those who had faith. They key component here is the faith of Jesus's followers. It was their faith that led to their immediate recovery. As you may recall in Mark 6:5, Jesus couldn't perform miracles in his hometown of Nazareth, outside of laying his hands on a few sick people. Why could he not perform his miraculous healing in Nazareth? Of course, it was their unbelief. Yes, God offers divine healing to all of us; however, we must first believe in him and his healing.

> Mark 6:5 - And he could do no mighty work there, except that he laid his hands upon a few sick people and healed them.

So where are you on the Jesus belief scale? Do you believe, really believe he will heal you when you reach out to him? Yet, is there still pain in your heart? In your life? Is the healing you seek not showing up completely in your life? I am going to guess that there is still pain in your life. There is still pain in mine. We both know that there is still pain in the world. However, since you are reading this book, I am going to also guess that you hold some level of belief in the healing powers of Jesus.

Well, at this point we know that the Evil One is the ruler of this world and he is wreaking havoc as he prowls about. However, we also know that Jesus Christ has already conquered him and he, the One dwelling within you, has greater power than the one who is in the world. In light of these truths, we also know that there is much suffering in the world. So what is mankind missing?

TIME TO CHART A NEW PATH

Since we know Jesus is trustworthy and he delivers what he promises, maybe we are not trusting the instruction he is giving us. Maybe he is speaking to humanity, and we are too stuck in our own ways to embrace his ways. The Holy Spirit dwells within us, and the Holy Spirit provides humanity with the instruction needed for complete and total world transformation. This instruction is already alive in the hearts and souls of God's children.

> *1 Corinthians 12:5-11 - To one is given through the*
> *Spirit the utterance of wisdom, and to another the*
> *utterance of knowledge according to the same*
> *Spirit, to another faith by the same Spirit, to*
> *another gifts of healing by the one Spirit, to*
> *another the working of miracles, to another*
> *prophecy, to another the ability to distinguish*
> *between spirits, to another various kinds of*
> *tongues, to another the interpretation of tongues.*
> *All these are inspired by one and the same Spirit,*
> *who apportions to each one individually as he wills.*

Albert Einstein - Insanity: Doing the same thing over and over and expecting different results.

We know we need to chart a new path if we are to realize and live the life of our dreams. Looking around the world, we witness many seeking to do this very thing through a plethora of religions and philosophies. However, we must be ever mindful that Jesus alone is fully human and fully divine, and it is he alone who said he is the way, the truth, and the life.

> *John 14:6 - Jesus said to him, "I am the way, and the*
> *truth, and the life; no one comes to the Father, but*
> *by me."*

Jesus alone stands at the right hand of God in all his fullness, and this includes his human nature. Yes, human nature now stands at the right hand of God, and this is why Jesus Christ is our one and only way into heaven. Although many of the world's religions and philosophies can offer positive instruction and guidance, I believe that no other priest, prophet, avatar, deity, or leader can do for us what Jesus Christ can do – lead us to the source of all peace, love and happiness. Not Buddha, not Muhammad, not Lao Tzu, no oneness thought leader or mindfulness guru can do for humanity what Jesus can and does do. I am by no means trying to take away from the beauty found in these other religions and philosophies. Being a Naturopath I have witnessed the transformational power they hold in the lives of others. However, the truth remains, all healing comes to us from God, through his Son, and in the Holy Spirit. I believe our Triune God meets us where we are and that he has many ways of communicating with mankind. After all, God is infinite and limitless. He is not bound to the constraints of time and space that our physical world is subject too.

THE JESUS CODE CONNECTION
Holistic Healing – Christ Healing

FINDING A NEW WAY IN THIS TROUBLED WORLD

Miracles are happing in the world right now, both big and small. To develop a deeper understanding of the miraculous world we live in, I invite you into the world of our saints: men and women who have found Jesus in a very profound and beautiful way. Here are a few of my favorites – great bedtime reading.

- Saint Teresa of Avila, Carmelite
- Saint John of the Cross, Carmelite
- Thomas Merton, OCSO
- Meister Eckhart, O.P.
- Saint Catherine of Siena, TOSD
- Saint Francis of Assisi, OFM
- Julia of Norwich, Anchoress
- Fr. Richard Rohr, OFM

So now imagine for a moment what the world would look like if all of mankind lived by Jesus's two commandments: love God above all other gods and love our brother as ourselves. Imagine the difference this would make in your life, in your family's life. The earth, then filled with hope, love, and life, would spontaneously support a life of happiness and peace for all. The truth is that God will walk the earth with mankind again, he will reclaim his creation, and Jesus Christ will come again. However, before this happens, mankind must be cleansed of sin and pain, and this is where you come in. You can participate in God's divine plan by allowing him to heal your brokenness and your pain.

> *Revelation 21:3 - I heard a loud shout from the throne saying, "Look, the home of God is now among men, and he will live with them and they will be his people; yes, God himself will be among them."*

THE JESUS CODE CONNECTION
Love – Power

TIME TO CHART A NEW COURSE

We need to chart a new course—we need to find another way. After all, our Christian history is full of misdirected actions and cruel behavior, often in the name of our Savior. Remember, we are called to love—that's all. We are called to love God above all gods, and we are called to love our brother as ourselves. It is time for God's children to reach their fullest potential; however, a change of heart is required. We must support healing modalities that embrace deeper healing, even when they appear non-conventional to our eyes. After all, Jesus certainly was not conventional in his healing nor did he follow man's law. He followed God's law, and multitudes were healed.

Luke 6:19 - And the people all tried to touch him, because power was coming from him and healing them all.

LIVE LANGUAGE

When writing this book I had one objective in mind. To help you, my reader, overcome the internal blocks holding you back from experiencing all the happiness and peace God offers. To accomplish this I will guide you through what I have dubbed LIVE Language. This language consists of LIVE Statements. These statements are crafted to transform your inner subconscious files that are not congruent with peace and happiness. Words are powerful, and words of truth will free you from the patterns that are not congruent with the life God offers.

Your LIVE Statements will arise as you dive deep into the Nine Faces of Struggle and face what Saint Teresa of Avila calls your reptiles – the creatures living in the mote around your castle. Inside your castle is the Throne Room – the space where your soul meets with God's perfect love. In the Throne Room you experience infinite peace and happiness. And to borrow from the thought of Meister Eckhart, in this space you will come into contact with God's ground – the place of your bliss.

THE NINE FACES OF STRUGGLE

Over my many years of practice, I have observed nine universal themes where individuals tend to get stuck in their lives, themes that lead to physical, emotional, and spiritual pain when not addressed. Such subsequent pain can reside in your body, heart, or soul, and I have come to believe that this pain is primarily the result of transgenerational entanglements and the false beliefs that follow. All of these issues have a hand in the working of your subconscious mind. In order to turn this kind of heartache around you must grasp an understanding of the power they hold in your life and your power to overcome them with truth. By utilizing The Jesus Code and

LIVE Language, I believe you can move beyond The Nine Faces of Struggle and experience happiness and peace.

THE NINE FACES OF STRUGGLE

1. Emotions – Creator of Disease or Health
2. The Seven Stages of Healing
3. The Pain of Exclusion in The Family
4. Forgiveness of Self and Others
5. Overcoming Childhood Wounds
6. Father as Provider and Protector
7. Anxiety and Depression
8. Addictions, Religion and God
9. Mother as Nurturer and Comforter

In the chapters that follow, you will undoubtedly see yourself and your loved ones in and between the lines. I invite you to welcome God into your heart as you read this book and listen to the message he has for you. As you read and understand The Nine Faces of Struggle, you will be presented with many opportunities to examine your subconscious mind as you uncover insights about your life and the world around you. I invite you to share with yourself what arises in your body, heart, and soul as your read and contemplate what has been penned here.

> Isaiah 42:16 - "I will lead the blind by a road they do not know, by paths they have not known I will guide them. I will turn the darkness before them into light, the rough places into level ground. These are the things I will do, and I will not forsake them."

THE JESUS CODE CONNECTION
Transform – Overcome - Transcend

« Chapter 4 »

The LIVE Method

Saint Mother Teresa of Calcutta - "Kind words can be short and easy to speak, but their echoes are truly endless."

Before we dive into The Nine Faces of Struggle, let's jump forward to the transformation piece and explain how real transformation happens. After all, real healing and transformation are what each and every one of us seeks throughout our lifetime. It is undoubtedly the reason you are reading this book. As I have shared with you, I have spent decades seeking and searching for truth. My own pain has been the catalyst. All of this seeking has led to the creation of The LIVE Method a modality that uses forgiveness and acceptance in a Christian setting to bring about transformation so that individuals can fully live and experience the fullness of love. In addition to LIVE Language, Family Constellations and the Enneagram are central components to The LIVE Method as well.

FAMILY CONSTELLATIONS

Family Constellations, a term coined by Bert Hellinger, is a modality that offers a transgenerational lens to reveal and transform subconscious thought patterns that hold us back from peace and happiness. The word constellation itself is a term used in medicine and psychology when referring to a group of symptoms or diseases. In this work we are looking at the symptoms and patterns found in families passed down through the generations.

When combined with LIVE, Family Constellations can be experienced three different ways; on your own, in a private session, or in a group setting. All three approaches are effective, powerful, and can be life changing. Throughout the rest of this book I will reference all three approaches.

1) Self-LIVE. On your own you identify the family members where hurt exists and you can either hold them in your heart as you say your LIVE Statements, or you can use figurines set out on a table before you. I often use practice Self-LIVE without figurines when I sit in the chapel at my church and pray for my family. In Chapter 14 I will show you how to craft your own Self-LIVE statements.

2) Private Sessions. With the guidance of a LIVE Practitioner you will place figurines that represent your family members on a table or desk in front of you. These will be the family members where hurt exists in your heart – you know, where the work needs to be done. Most often the figurines will be placed at a distance apart. Your practitioner will then guide you through LIVE Statements. Together with your practitioner you will move the figurines as you feel a movement in your heart. You will be surprised to see how easy it becomes to move the figurines close together as the session unfolds.

3) Retreat Setting. In a retreat setting the attendees have the opportunity to have their Family Constellation done in a group setting. During this process the client, under the guidance of the facilitator, will ask other retreat attendees to stand in, or proxy, for their family members. The facilitator will then guide each individual through LIVE Statements created to bring about respite in the heart of the client. Like the private sessions, you will be surprised how good your heart feels when your "family members" move around the space as the session unfolds.

THE ENNEAGRAM

At the time of the writing of the first edition of *Understanding The Jesus Code* I was unfamiliar with the Enneagram, a tool that I now use extensively in my LIVE work. On my continued search for truth I was lead to the work of Father Rich Rohr, OFM, a Franciscan priest who's thought I find captivating. As I became familiar with his work I came across a book he had written, *The Enneagram: A Christian Perspective*. The Enneagram opened up a whole new range of possibilities for my work. Looking at transformation through the lens of the Enneagram requires a look at the internal subconscious files that come "pre-loaded" in our psyche.

While *Understanding The Jesus Code* is not an exploration into the Enneagram, that is another book percolating inside my heart and mind, a brief introduction into its wisdom is essential. To begin, I recommend you find out what Enneagram type you identify with – there are nine different types. You can either take the Enneagram test at Enneagraminstitute.com or you can pick up a good book on the topic. Father Richard Rohr's book is an excellent guide on this note. Additionally, my website TheLIVEMethod.com offers information on the Enneagram you will find helpful

In a nut shell, the Enneagram offers insight into the internal voice inside of us. And most importantly, it reveals to us our spiritual path towards wholeness. Each of the nine types have their own path. Whereas LIVE offers a tool to tear down the hurdles to wholeness, the Enneagram reveals to us the direction our path is leading us on.

This internal voice has been with us since our conception - it is how we experience God's love and beauty. This voice helps create the roadmap on our spiritual journey. The Enneagram's nine different types are personality types of sort. However, much more than a personality system, the Enneagram helps identify your spiritual personality alongside with your spiritual journey.

Have you ever wondered why children who were raised in the same family, even twins, can be so different? The Enneagram helps explain this. Each type has different core fears and expressions of love. For example, Type Two, which I identify with, has a core need to be loved and we express this need through loving and helping others. Loving and helping others is an intrinsic desire Type Twos naturally embody. As they heal from their wounds they can become very helpful servants in the world. Type One in the other hand, the type my husband identifies with, has a core need to be good. You can always count on a Type One to do the right thing – whatever they view to be the right thing. They will strive for perfection and they are very demanding on themselves. As Type One individuals heal from their inner wounds they become champions for good in the world, reformers who seek to make the world a better, more perfect, place.

With LIVE, grasping an understanding of your inner voice is essential to transformation and knowing what Enneagram type you identify with is a foundational piece on this journey.

THE LIVE METHOD

So how does The LIVE Method work? To begin, at its core, the perfect love of Christ is acknowledged as the sole healing tonic available to mankind and in order to fully live we must allow his love free reign in our body, heart, and soul. The intention of LIVE is to clear the blocks that interfere with love and allow love to heal as only perfect love can.

With LIVE, we acknowledge that all life has been passed on to us through our ancestral lineage—beginning with our first parents, who were created in the likeness and image of God himself, and I'll add here that God said that this creation of his was *very* good.

> *Genesis 1:31 - And God saw everything that he had made, and behold, it was very good. And there was evening and there was morning, a sixth day.*

However, bad things have happened throughout the history of humanity; mankind has sinned, and this limits our happiness today. This sin has separated your ancestors from fully living, and this sin has led to the creation of subconscious files that are not congruent with God's plans for your life.

Looking back to Adam and Eve, we can see this truth. Adam and Eve both felt shame and fear after the Fall, didn't they? However, how did God respond to them? Yes, like any good father, he allowed discipline; however, if you are a parent, you can understand that this hurt God much more than it hurt Adam and Eve. Yet through it all, God loved them, and he still loves all of humanity. You see, the truth is that God desired to love Adam and Eve even when they didn't feel worthy, their beliefs were not congruent with God's love for them, and it was their beliefs that kept them separate from God's love. You and I are still living in the same paradigm when we hold on to false beliefs and it is these beliefs that need to be transformed so that love can enter in and transform us.

> *John 3:16 - For God so loved the world that he gave his only Son, that whoever believes in him should not perish but have eternal life.*

THE JESUS CODE CONNECTION
Restoration

HOW DO WE MOVE FORWARD AND FULLY LIVE?

With LIVE, the goal is to restore love and transform false and limiting beliefs. While there tends to be a significant amount of talk about limiting beliefs these days, much of this chatter doesn't go to the root cause of these beliefs. Given this, one can enter into the merry-go-round of healing, a merry-go-round where many find themselves moving from one modality to another seeking fulfillment. My friends, the root is the Fall of our first parents, and there is only one way back to full restoration. You must go back through your ancestral lineage and unlock the limiting beliefs that sin created in you and your family, with the help of Jesus Christ. You must forgive those who have harmed you, including your parents, and you must accept the circumstances of your life as it is.

But wait, you may be saying, "Whoa there, Carolyn!" Back up the bus and wait a minute. I can't forgive; it's too hard, and there is no way I am going to accept what has happened to me. You don't understand my life and the path I have walked. Agreed, I don't know your path; however, I have been around long enough to understand the real sense of pain individuals experience in this world. Additionally, I also know the power Jesus holds in our lives. I understand this sounds difficult.

Let's stop for a moment and ponder what it would feel like if you experienced forgiveness for those who have hurt you. How light would your heart feel? What would it feel like if you were able to experience acceptance of the truth about your life as it is? When you can't accept some portion of your life you are likely focused on some aspect of your past. For example. Let's say you wish you had different parents – perhaps kinder and more loving parents. A lot of individuals hold on to this wish. When you hold on to this wish you tend to ruminate over the past. You find yourself wishing life would have been different, believing that life would be better with different parents. This gives power to a life that never happened – and will never happen. A rather hopeless dream to hold on to. The truth is that you have the parents you have, this cannot be changed. What you can change is the thought you have about your life as it is and the direction you want it to go.

When you hold on to a life that doesn't exist you limit your potential for abundance and happiness right now. Think for a moment how free you would feel if you could be present now without dragging the past into today. How free would you be if you could move forward with renewed enthusiasm for today and tomorrow without dragging the weight of yesterday?

> Jesus will never allow you to take on more than you can handle.

It takes a lot of energy to stand in unforgiveness and unacceptance. It is a painful place to be, and the Evil One wants to hold you there. I say his days are limited, and it's time for us to reclaim our birthright! However, this is where I also said there would be bumps and challenges along the way. By utilizing LIVE you will find a way through your limiting beliefs. These are the beliefs holding you trapped in unforgiveness and unacceptance. Before you can step into a new life you must first wade into the waters of your life experiences. The beautiful piece here is the fact that Jesus Christ, the one who loves and knows you beyond all measure, will guide you perfectly. Remember he is at the center of LIVE, and for good reason—this is serious work. Jesus will never allow you to take on more than you can handle. Once you have transformed your limiting beliefs your life will be forever changed. New beliefs of abundance, happiness, and peace will direct your body, heart, and soul. You will step into your true inheritance as a child of God. This inheritance is what you will then pass on to your children, the generations that follow, and into the world. Trust me—it's worth the ride.

> *Psalm 139:13 - For thou didst form my inward parts, thou didst knit me together in my mother's womb.*

As you read through The Nine Faces of Struggle, I will share with you beliefs that my clients and I have transformed into truth. Undoubtedly, you will see yourself and your family in many of the stories, because through it all we are all a part of the same body. As each part of this body heals, the whole body becomes restored.

> *1 Corinthians 12:12 - For just as the body is one and has many members, and all the members of the body, though many, are one body, so it is with Christ.*

THE JESUS CODE CONNECTION
Forward – New Life

« Chapter 5 »

The 1st Face of Struggle: Emotions— Creator of Disease?

Thomas Merton - "Love is our true destiny. We do not find the meaning of life by ourselves alone - we find it with another."

Being human calls you to experience the world in a sea of emotions. Some are life-giving, while others have stolen segments of your life from you. If you desire to live a life of abundance, happiness, and peace, you must first understand how your emotions impact your ability to do so, and most importantly, you must find a way to address painful emotions so they can be transformed. Understanding your Enneagram type will serve you in this area. Each Enneagram type carries an underlying dominant emotion. When you are under stress you will tend towards the emotion associated with your type. For example, types Eight, Nine, and One tend towards anger when they are under stress. Whereas types Two, Three, and Four tend towards shame. And types Five, Six, and Seven tend towards anxiety. While each of us will experience anger, shame, and anxiety there lies within a tendency to lean a certain way based on the Enneagram type we identify with. Understanding your unique internal voice, and the emotions that follow, is central to transformation. This voice is a combination of your life experiences, inherited tendencies, and interactions with others - all experienced through the lens of your Enneagram type.

To ignore or deny painful emotions only serves to set the stage for an emotional eruption or a disease state at some point in the future. Your body cannot ignore emotional distress any more than it can ignore the physical touch of a burning stove. You must either process the emotional pain in a timely manner or run the risk of burying the pain in your tissues. Whims of uncontrolled anger, shame, or anxiety experienced today most often find their impetus in previously experienced events in our lives. Undoubtedly, you have found it is almost unbearable to look behind the veil of anger, resentment, or fear without feeling shame and regret. However, no matter how painful life can be, you are never alone left without help. God has promised that he will strengthen you, he will help you, and he has told you that you do not need to be afraid.

> *Isaiah 41:10 - "'Fear not, for I am with you. Do not be dismayed. I am your God. I will strengthen you; I will help you; I will uphold you with my victorious right hand.'"*

There is much more to this life than you could possible imagine, and you can use your emotions as a road map to reach the ultimate joy, peace and love your heart craves.

However; fear and other painful emotions are very real when you are experiencing them. By utilizing LIVE Language, you can move beyond painful emotions. Painful emotions cannot coexist with love and therefore they must be addressed before you can live a life of happiness. In this chapter on emotions and disease, you will dive into the sea of emotions as you become aware of the power they hold in your physical, emotional, and spiritual body. Modern science today is rich with studies revealing the power emotions hold over your attempt to obtain good health, and this is a wonderful advancement. There is much more to this life than you could possibly imagine, and you can use your emotions as a road map to reach the ultimate life your heart craves. And those painful emptions, well, they can provide the perfect catalyst into wholeness when we choose to move through them and transform the root pattern they were born out of.

James 1:19-21 - You must understand this, my beloved: let everyone be quick to listen, slow to speak, slow to anger; for your anger does not produce God's righteousness. Therefore rid yourselves of all sordidness and rank growth of wickedness, and welcome with meekness the implanted word that has the power to save your souls.

THE JESUS CODE CONNECTION
Emotions – Anger – Shame – Fear

EMOTIONS AND YOUR BODY

> If your parents and grandparents experienced significant stressors in their lives this could have a significant negative effect on your DNA.

As I mentioned, modern science is looking at the intimate connection between your emotions and disease. You may be surprised to learn that the emotions your ancestors experienced not only changed their DNA and biochemistry, but studies now show that this changed DNA is also passed onto subsequent generations when extreme trauma is experienced. Yes, you heard that correct. If your parents and grandparents experienced significant stressors in their lives, this could have a significant negative effect on your DNA.

Let's look at studies conducted by the HeartMath Institute in California regarding our hearts and emotions. With the use of EKGs (electrocardiographs, which are instruments that record the electrical activity of the heart) and EEGs (electroencephalographs, which record the electrical activity of the brain), scientists have observed that the heart's electrical activity is significantly greater than the electrical activity of the brain. Let's reflect for a moment on this. Our heart's energy is bigger than our brain's energy. Given this, shouldn't we be paying significant attention to our heart and the message it has for us? You know, our inner voice, our intuition? Yet, how many of us today walk around thinking, planning, and applying logic to our lives? Now, I am not saying it is bad to use our brain, quite the contrary. God gave us a human brain for a reason and it can accomplish great things! I for one am grateful for the mind that created the computer I used to create this book. However, the modern person seems to have lost touch with their heart. We are a thinking generation, we have to see the proof, we have to see the science, and we highly value logic and reason to the point of idolizing it.

All the while we are missing the sweet spot! Our hearts hold our greatest power because they hold the healing emotion of love. Perhaps we hold our greatest power in our hearts because it is in our heart that Jesus lives. However, to trust in the power of our heart requires faith in a world beyond the world we know now, a world that we can come to know through our heart.

> *Hebrews 11:1-3 - Now faith is the assurance of things hoped for, the conviction of things not seen. Indeed, by faith our ancestors received approval. By faith we understand that the worlds were prepared by the word of God, so that what is seen was made from things that are not visible.*

There was another study done at Mount Sinai's Traumatic Stress Division on the DNA changes resulting from the extreme trauma endured by Holocaust survivors. What the team found with these 32 men and women may surprise you. A marker attached to the DNA of the survivors as a result of the trauma of the Holocaust. In turn this marker altered their DNA. Additionally, this altered DNA was then passed down to their children. This is called epigenetic inheritance – the idea that one's environment imparts a change in DNA and this new DNA is then passed down to the children and grandchildren. So my thought is this - if science already reveals to us the negative change trauma has on our DNA and the DNA we pass on to the generations that follow us, is it possible that we can positively affect our DNA and pass a healthier DNA down to our children and the generations that follow? My reply is a resounding YES!

> Ezekiel 18:14, 17 - "But if this man begets a son who sees all the sins which his father has done, and fears, and does not do likewise . . . [who] withholds his hand from iniquity, takes no interest or increase, observes my ordinances, and walks in my statutes; he shall not die for his father's iniquity; he shall surely live.

THE JESUS CODE CONNECTION
DNA – New Life

BRAINS, EMOTIONS AND CHEMISTRY

Let's chat a little bit about your central nervous system, with a discussion about neuropeptides. Neuropeptides, chemical messengers in the body, team up with various biochemicals including serotonin, GABA, dopamine, and other biochemicals that all contribute to how you feel. When neuropeptides are released during emotions such as anger, shame, or anxiety they lock into a very specific pattern reflective of these emotions. The more you experience a particular emotion the deeper set this configuration becomes in your body's organs. This also holds true for emotions such as love, joy, and peace. Think of this mechanism akin to grooves in a record that has been played over and over again. Eventually, the grooves become rather deep. When you experience repeated emotions, your body behaves in a similar manner. If you have a long history of harmful emotions, then when life throws you a curveball, your knee-jerk reaction will be to experience harmful emotions again and again—unless you do something to interrupt this pattern.

Ephesians 3:16-17 - I pray that, according to the riches of his glory, he may grant that you may be strengthened in your inner being with power through his Spirit, and that Christ may dwell in your hearts through faith, as you are being rooted and grounded in love.

THE JESUS CODE CONNECTION
Pattern Interrupt – Choose Love

YOUR SYMPATHETIC VS. PARASYMPATHETIC NERVOUS SYSTEM

Let's look briefly at your response to stress and how it affects your system in another way—the parasympathetic and sympathetic components of your nervous system. Consider for a moment your ability to fight or flight when exposed to a stressor. During exposure to a threatening stressor, your body will engage your sympathetic system—your fight or flight system. At this point, your body is sending most of its energy to your large muscle groups and your cardiovascular system so that you can take action. Stress hormones are released throughout your system, and your adrenals are switched into high gear. Needless to say, at this point, your body is not in a position to repair or heal itself. It is focused with survival.

Your mind doesn't differentiate between real or perceived stress – they are one in the same.

A quick look at the world today and we can see that stress is the cause of many of our modern-day diseases. We are a group of people running on adrenaline! Your body responds to stress when you are actually in the stressful moment *and* when you are thinking about a stressor. That's right, the cascade of stress hormones that are released when you are actually thinking about the stressful situation is the same cascade that are released during the actual event. Your mind doesn't differentiate between real or perceived stress – they are one in the same. One more reason to not watch scary movies and to extend forgiveness towards those who harm you.

So when does your body heal itself? Healing and regeneration occur when your parasympathetic system is engaged. This happens during prayer, meditation, relaxation, and when the body is at peace. Additionally, while in a parasympathetic state, your body can digest your food optimally. Meal time can be one of the most healing moments in our lives, providing we take our time to enjoy our meal and engage in heartfelt conversation with those around our table.

It's obviously important to incorporate daily activities where you can enjoy yourself, whether that's reading, playing, praying, or spending time with your loved ones. I invite you to find a morning routine that sets a healthy intention for the day, one that is grounded in Christ. I also invite you to find a new way to deal with life's stressors. When I am upset, I often go to the perpetual adoration chapel at my parish and spend some time with Our Lord in prayer.

> Healing and regeneration occur when your parasympathetic system is engaged. This happens during prayer, meditation, relaxation, and when the body is at peace.

1 Peter 5:6, 7 - Humble yourselves therefore under the mighty hand of God, that in due time he may exalt you. Cast all your anxieties on him, for he cares about you.

If he who is in the world, Satan, created the trauma and pain that led to all the above mentioned physical and emotional responses, then do you believe that the One who lives within you, Jesus Christ, has the power to heal your pain? Of course he does, and since this healing hasn't happened on a large, worldwide scale, we know that humanity has not yet found the right path for healing.

THE JESUS CODE CONNECTION
Choose Another Way

THE COMPLEXITIES OF ANGER

Anger and worry present unique challenges for men and women. While both emotions are experienced by each gender (and all Enneagram types), the experience is different for the sexes. Let's start by looking at anger. At its core, anger is an acquired protective measure you take on when hurt has occurred as a result of unrequited love. When you repeatedly extend love to another, especially your parents in your early childhood, and love is not returned, a wound inside your heart and soul is created. If the experience is perpetuated the wound deepens and it becomes buried deeper and deeper within. As a child, expressing anger toward your parents was an impossible thought for many reasons and, given this, another solution must be sought. Sadly, burying anger is often the only solution children have available to them.

Anger is also the response for adults who have buried wounds. Like a pressure cooker, at some point buried anger has to come out. This is even true for those who do not identify with Enneagram types Eight, Nine, or One. If you remember, these are the Enneagram types that tend to lean into anger when they are stressed. As someone who identifies with Enneagram Two, the type who leans into shame under stress, I can personally attest to this "leaning". In the past when I was trapped in my wounds I would often tell myself "I'm not good enough", "Other people are better than me.", "I am inherently flawed." etc. – all of this fits with Enneagram Two. However, I also held anger in my heart for way to many years, anger that I buried time and time again when I extended love and it wasn't returned. This anger interfered with the greatest gift an Enneagram Two has to offer the world – the gift of love. Who can feel loved when they are around someone who is angry – no one really. It's not that I was angry all the time; however, my internal anger certainly held me back from loving others and being loved in return. Further, it contributed to my shame. After I expressed anger I felt horrible about myself and I sunk deeper into my shame.

Let's look at the two primary reasons anger is such a powerful force in our lives. First, when biochemicals associated with anger are released, a sense of empowerment rushes through the body—many have become addicted to such a rush. Secondly, anger serves to keep others at a distance, far enough away so that the pain of unrequited love, and its tears, is safely hidden from others. You see, whenever a harmful emotion like anger shows up, we know there is hurt underneath that resulted from a separation with love. Out of fear, both conscious and unconscious, you will hide this hurt from the world.

MEN, WOMEN, AND ANGER

Let's look at how anger functions differently in men and women. I invite you to think for a moment what a man needs to do when his family is under attack—think cave man here. He needs to step into immediate action, and anger serves to facilitate this end. Once the battle is won and all is well, his anger is no longer needed, and he can calm down, which he does rather quickly.

Women also experience anger; however, their experience is different. Women are generally the ones who keep the family closely knit together because we tend to be more relational in nature. Also, traditionally, women are the ones who look after small children. A quick anger switch wouldn't serve either role for women. Remember, anger serves to create walls and block the flow of love. When anger builds in a woman, it eventually comes out as an eruption—leaving many a man perplexed. In the past, this was indeed my pattern. However, instead of burying grievances, I now go to prayer and allow Jesus to transform my heart. Given that Mother Mary has a mother's compassionate heart, I often seek her intercession in these instances. My heart then becomes filled with compassion, understanding, and forgiveness. What follows are more Godly relationships in my life. My Enneagram Two starts to shine.

> Ephesians 4:26-27, 29 - "Be angry but do not sin;"
> do not let the sun go down on your anger, and do
> not make room for the devil . . . Let no evil talk
> come out of your mouths, but only what is useful
> for building up, as there is need, so that your words
> may give grace to those who hear.

WORRY NO MORE

Now let's chat about worry. While both sexes worry, we tend to think of worry as more of a female issue—to which I agree. I invite you to ponder for a moment the woman's primary role in the family. She is the comforter and the nurturer, the one who God has blessed with the ability to care for and nurture a baby within her body for nine months and then nourish for many more months (years) after the birth. While men can certainly comfort and nurture children, they often find more enjoyment meeting a child's need for play and adventure.

There is a saying that goes like this: "Moms comfort and dads poke." There is some significant truth in this. Moms create comfort in the home, and dads prepare children to go out into the world. Given a woman's role as comforter and nurturer, would it serve the family if mom went to anger quickly like a man? Of course not. Yet she does need to be ever vigilant about the activity of the little ones around her. Worry helps her keep a watchful eye. Yes, mom does need to sweat the small stuff sometimes—especially if a child has put themselves in imminent danger. The challenge for a women is to not allow worry to consume her heart to the point of limiting the full expression of God's love through her.

Jesus promised us that he offers peace beyond what the world offers. Given this, for those suffering from excessive worry, we know freedom is possible. I believe it is time for us to discover a new way into freedom because, for billions of people across the world, what we are doing right now simply isn't working.

> Jesus promised us that he offers peace beyond what the world offers.

Philippians 4:6-7 - Have no anxiety about anything, but in everything by prayer and supplication with thanksgiving let your requests be made known to God. And the peace of God, which passes all understanding, will keep your hearts and your minds in Christ Jesus.

THE JESUS CODE CONNECTION
Surrender Anger – Surrender Anxiety

GUILT AND SHAME

Both guilt and shame have the power to block your heart from experiencing the fullness of happiness, peace, and the love your heart desires. Yet, they are both very different. Guilt is more transitory in nature whereas shame is more damaging to your heart and soul. Guilt is experienced when you acknowledge you did something wrong; however, you still see yourself as a lovable person. You just made a mistake. Shame, on the other hand, leads you to believe you are inherently flawed. Shame is indeed very heavy to carry around.

"Susan"

A while back I had a client in my office I will call Susan. Susan and I had been working together for years on her nutritional needs with rather good success; however, she was struggling with her relationship with her boss, so she wanted to start addressing the emotional component to her well-being. Susan was a front office employee at a medical office, and her boss, who I will call Jennifer, was the office manager. During her LIVE session, Susan confessed to me that she really didn't like Jennifer and she found herself struggling with forgiving this woman for some rather hurtful comments that she had made concerning Susan's effectiveness at work. Jennifer was one of those difficult-to-live-with individuals in Susan's life, and since Susan is on her journey toward greater well-being, she is trying to love and forgive Jennifer.

However, Susan finds forgiveness and love nearly impossible when Jennifer is curt and rude—which seems to be often. After further discussion, Susan shared with me that her dad had coached many of her volleyball teams as a child and he had been particularly critical of her after the games on their ride home. This was Susan's first recollection of criticism in her life, so we decided to use this life experience as a springboard for the session.

Susan was experiencing guilt and not shame for not being able to forgive Jennifer. We discovered this to be true because Susan didn't believe she was inherently bad for not being able to forgive Jennifer. She knew she could forgive her and she knew she would be able to figure this out. However, at Susan's core, Jennifer's cutting words about her work performance made Susan *believe* she was not good at her job, i.e., she felt shame about her work performance because she *believed* she was flawed. Even though she admitted that she did a good job, she went on and listed several reasons why she wasn't capable of doing it well—none of which made sense to me as I sat and listened at her. To me, Susan came across as a competent, trustworthy employee who did her job well.

Below are a few healing statements that empowered Susan, helped her to release guilt and shame, and helped her move into a life of greater happiness and peace. Most importantly, they helped her reach her goal of forgiving and loving Jennifer and herself. As a bonus, her relationship with her father improved greatly. Not only did she begin to feel gratitude for all the time he put into coaching her, she became excited to spend with him again.

Note: In Chapter 14, "The Language of LIVE Within The Nine Faces of Struggle," we will go into great detail on how to create specific transformation statements for your personal journey. For now, I invite you to read and enjoy Susan's story. With that being said, you may want to reflect back on Susan's statements once you have worked through Chapter 14.

Key Forgiveness Statements

- I forgive myself for believing I can't forgive Jennifer.

- I forgive myself for believing that forgiving Jennifer needs to be hard.

- I forgive myself for believing I can't feel competent when I am near Jennifer.

- I forgive myself for believing that if I forgive Jennifer, then she gets away with the pain she has caused me.

- I forgive myself for believing I can't look at Jennifer without remembering all the times she has hurt me.

- I forgive myself for believing I can't enjoy my job when Jennifer is present.

- I forgive myself for believing that when Jennifer speaks to me about my job I have to be the child I was when I was playing volleyball and my dad was my coach.

- I forgive my dad for anything he has ever said or done while coaching me that made me feel I wasn't good enough.

- I forgive my dad for anything he has ever said or done while coaching me that made me feel I wasn't a great volleyball player.

Key Dad Statements

- I take from my relationship with my dad what is best for my spiritual growth as God desires, and I leave what is not best for me with Jesus to do with as he desires.

- I proclaim that the experiences I shared with my dad when he coached me only serve to bring me closer to God.

- I give gratitude for the coaching my dad gave me, and I acknowledge that my dad is the right dad for me.

Key Empowering Spiritual and Permission Statements

- I acknowledge the shame I feel when I believe I am not a competent employee, and I lay it at the foot of the cross for Jesus to heal it. I ask God, through Jesus and in the Holy Spirit, to come into that space and heal it, turn it around so I can more fully express my gifts in my work as God intends.

- I give myself permission to accept that the way my dad coached me was perfect for the growth of my heart and soul.

- I give myself permission to accept that no matter what my dad or Jennifer may say about my performance, their words do not have the power to separate me from fulfilling the intention God has for my life.

- I give myself permission to accept that my dad coached me the best he knew how and his coaching was right for me.

- I give myself permission to feel and enjoy the love my dad had for me and I give his love greater power in my life than his criticism.

THE JESUS CODE CONNECTION
Forgiveness – Acceptance – Earthly father

After Susan's session, her heart toward both her dad and Jennifer felt significantly lighter. She shared with me that when she was around Jennifer, she no longer felt inadequate and she was able to receive Jennifer's criticism as constructive. She also later shared with me that shortly after her session, her dad reached out with an invitation to attend an Indianapolis Indians baseball game. She accepted the invitation, and they had a great day together— something she would have not been able to do before without feeling a sense of inadequacy. Beautiful!

You see, with Susan, her guilt made it hard for her to forgive. She felt bad about not being able to forgive, yet she knew she was capable of offering forgiveness. As guilt goes, she didn't believe that her unforgiveness was a character flaw, because she knew she was capable of extending it.

However, her shame in the belief that she was incompetent was found at the root of her pain. Once Susan was able to release her shame, forgiveness came easier. Now when Jennifer offers criticism, Susan views it in a different light. No longer does she feel like the incompetent volleyball player of her youth (which she wasn't – she received many awards!). She is able to even counter Jennifer's criticism in a constructive way that facilitates constructive dialog. Further, Susan was able to accept her relationship wither her father as it is, acknowledging in her heart that her father was doing the best he knew how to do throughout her life. She began to feel gratitude for his coaching, acknowledging that the other girls on the team didn't have fathers who extended this gift.

LET'S SIMPLIFY

Shame: When you actually believe you are inherently flawed or broken. An emotion that often has generational roots and it is especially rooted in Enneagram types Two, Three and Four individuals.

Guilt: When you know you did something wrong; however, you do not identify yourself as "bad" as a result.

> *Isaiah 43:18-19 - "Do not remember the former thing, or consider the things of old. I am about to do a new thing; now it springs forth, do you not perceive it? I will make a way in the wilderness and rivers in the desert."*

THE ENNEAGRAM TRIADS AND THE STRESS RESPONSE

Earlier we introduced the emotions different Enneagram types tend towards when under stress. Those in the Body Triad; types Eight, Nine, and One, tend towards anger. Those in the Head Triad; types Five, Six, and Seven, tend towards anxiety. And those in the Heart Triad; types Two, Three, and Four, tend towards shame when under stress. During our discussion on anger and anxiety we will take a deeper look into the response the Body and Head types exhibit. For now, let's discuss the Heart Triad.

First, let's begin our discussion what I mean when I use the word "stressed". While we often think of being stressed as a state of nervous energy or elevated uncomfortable excitability, its meaning here is a bit different. Here the word points to an emotional or physical state that takes us away from wholeness, periods of time when we move away from our true-self. You know, those moments when we don't feel quite right. Negative subconscious tapes that are not congruent with God's vision of ourselves keep playing in our mind. It is also important to recognize that stress is not always the result of our emotional state of mind. Dietary and lifestyle choices counter to health also find themselves at the root of stress in the body. Taking measures to care for your physical body by giving it right nourishment and movement is essential for wholeness.

For individuals in the Heart Triad, those who identify with Enneagram types Two, Three, or Four, their experience of shame stands at the forefront of their mind when they have moved off-center so to speak. While the other types also experience shame, types in the Heart Triad tend to own it in a very particular way.

While those in the Heart Triad, the feeling people, tend towards shame each type embodies it a bit differently. Type Two individuals go outward into the world to help and care for others. Nancy Reagan and Richard Thomas "John Boy Walton" are examples of Type Two individuals. They are empathetic and caring individuals who want to help others. Type Twos are relational in nature, and when they fall prey to shame they begin to falsely believe that they are less then, or somehow inferior to others. Their shame clouds their internal view of who they really are – a beloved child of God who is not only worthy of love, they are immersed in the milieu of God's love. Their greatest need is to be loved. This need is thwarted because their shame begins to make them believe they are not worthy of being loved. While they will believe others are worthy of being loved, somehow their perceived flaws make them un-loveable.

Type Three individuals are the world's success orientated people. They are charming and self-assured. They bring forth innovation and great ideas into the world. Within themselves they carry a basic desire to be valuable. Bill Clinton and Tom Cruise both exemplify Type Three individuals. However, when Type Threes fall into shame they begin to falsely believe they are worthless. Feelings of unworthiness are unacceptable for Type Threes. In an attempt to maintain a successful image they bury their emotions and soldier on when they experience shame. They begin to lie to themselves, and to others. Like the Emperor without clothes, type Threes find protection behind denial.

Type Four individuals are our sensitive creatives in the world who tend to go inward with their emotions. Think Edgar Allen Poe and Judy Garland here. They wear their emotions on their sleeves and they can be both dramatic and self-absorbed. They love beauty and they are very good at revealing God's beauty to the world. However, when they fall into shame they can enter into a downward emotional spiral leading them into self-indulgence and self-pity.

They become trapped in their painful emotions and they can easily find a sort of respite in these feelings. They need to feel and feelings congruent with depression or unworthiness can become an escape from the world. A shame filled Type Four individual will find themselves trapped when subconscious files of insignificance pillage their minds. Shame falsely convinces them that they have no intrinsic value. When this happens their belief that they are special and set apart for something magnificent shatters into a million pieces. What escapes them is the fact that they are indeed special and set aside for something beautiful in the eyes of God. We all are.

« Chapter 6 »

The 2nd Face of Struggle: The Seven Stages of Healing

Romans 5:3-5 - Knowing that suffering produces endurance, and endurance produces character, and character produces hope, and hope does not disappoint us, because God's love has been poured into our hearts through the Holy Spirit who has been given to us.

Have you ever considered why individuals exhibit markedly different responses to the same or similar situation? Why does one individual respond with anger while another responds with shame or anxiety? In addition to the impact our unique subconscious files have on our behavior (vis-a-vis our Enneagram type), we also experience life through a series of seven different emotional stages. In Kübler-Ross' model, the five stages of grief, we witness a series of these emotions. These stages include Denial, Anger, Bargaining, Depression, and Acceptance. Upon examination of these stages, we can see that individuals cycle through them throughout their life in an attempt to cope with the challenges life offers. In addition to the five stages offered by Kübler-Ross, two more stages can be found: "Love Entering In" and "Love Consuming." I call them "The Seven Stages of Healing."

THE SEVEN STAGES OF HEALING

1. Denial

2. Anger

3. Bargain

4. Depression

5. Acceptance

6. Love Entering In

7. Love Consuming

THE JESUS CODE CONNECTION
Suffering – Endurance – Hope in God

Regardless of what stage you are in at this time of your life, it is important to honor the fact that you exist where you are in an attempt to best cope with the struggles you have faced in your life up until this point. You are doing the best you can, given the load you are carrying—we all are. Additionally, it is through your struggles that the road map to happiness and peace will be found. However, before you can persevere on your journey, you must first develop an understanding of where you are, where you have been, and where you are going.

Once you understand how Denial is enlisted as a

> Regardless of what stage you are in at this time of your life, it is important to honor the fact that you exist where you are in an attempt to best cope with the struggles you have faced in your life up until this point.

protective shield, how the hedge of Anger holds you captive like a prisoner, what the false hope of Bargaining really costs you, and the how close you are to freedom while in the midst of Depression, you can then begin to experience real hope and believe that lasting happiness and peace are indeed available to you. Real hope enters into your heart as you begin to accept the truth of your life. Acceptance, in turn, opens the door for love to enter in and heal as only love can heal.

STAGE 1: DENIAL

> Everyone's threshold for stress is different, and modern science is now revealing that our stress barometer is intimately linked not only to our personal traumas but also to the generational traumas of those who came before us.

Let's begin with the coping mechanism of Denial. Individuals will enter into Denial in an attempt to deal with pain or trauma that is too much to handle. Individuals who have experienced earlier childhood trauma or PTSD (post-traumatic stress syndrome) frequently utilize Denial as an attempt to numb the pain. Given that modern science has now revealed that PTSD can adversely affect the DNA of subsequent generations, it is important that we address this coping mechanism effectively. Everyone's threshold for stress is different and modern science is now revealing that our stress barometer is intimately linked not only to our personal traumas but also to the generational traumas of those who came before us. Regardless of why someone is using Denial to cope with buried pain, it is important to respect the fact that they have experienced hurts in life beyond their ability to process them and move beyond.

So what does Denial look like? Denial can be virtually impossible to recognize to the inattentive eye because if you are in Denial, you are very good at acting like all is well. After all, this is how you have learned how to cope with pain. In an attempt to hide your pain from the world, you have mastered the art of burying it deep within. However, one of the tell-tale signs that you or a loved one are in Denial is a blunting of emotions—good and bad. To be fully alive promises us a beautiful range of emotional highs and lows in life. In Denial, you are not aware there is a problem, you have buried the trauma and its pain. This pattern will likely continue throughout your life unless this pattern is interrupted.

> Denial can be virtually impossible to recognize to the inattentive eye because if you are in Denial, you are very good at acting like all is well.

Matthew 14:27 - But immediately he (Jesus) spoke to them, saying, "Take heart, it is I; have no fear."

STAGE 2: ANGER

To begin, the stage of Anger is the beginning of feeling, and this can be a good thing. However, Anger takes a lot of energy, and it can be disastrous for your relationships if left to run wild. Think for a moment the last time you were angry. Perhaps you felt an empty sense of empowerment and control. How did that end up for you? Did this surge of energy nourish your relationships with your loved ones and others in the world? Did this surge of energy serve to strengthen your physical body? Or did your anger harm your relationships and tear down your physical body with the flooding of stress hormones? In the previous chapter, you learned about the unhealthy pattern of body chemicals that are released during anger. If you are looking to live life fully alive, then taking care of your relationships with others and your physical body are important components. And all this comes before we can even talk about using your divine gifts to work in unison with God and expand his kingdom!

There is a lot of finger pointing in Anger because there is a subconscious belief that someone, or something else, is the root of your pain. It is helpful to be mindful here that Anger is a coping mechanism often used as protection against the pain of not being loved. Often the object of unrequited love is your mother or father, as we will see in Chapters 10 and 13. As a child, if you experienced unrequited love with your parents, the subsequent pain likely cut deep into your being. Yet God, your ultimate parent, can and does fill in wherever your earthly parents cannot. He will supply all the strength you need when you turn to him.

> It is helpful to be mindful here that Anger is a coping mechanism often used as protection against the pain of not being loved by another.

Ephesians 6:10 - Finally, be strong in the Lord and in the strength of his might.

THE JESUS CODE CONNECTION
Coming Alive – Endurance

PARENTIFIED CHILDREN

God placed inside the human heart an ability to give and receive love so that love would expand between persons. In a healthy parent-child relationship this facilitates the expansion of love between them that sets the child on a path that will lead them into healthy relationships with others. However, when a parent is unable to give their child the love and care the child desires an imbalance occurs. In an attempt to restore love the child will sacrifice their own happiness if they believe this sacrifice will free their mom and dad to love them more. This dynamic can be especially troublesome when parents cannot fully take care of themselves, let alone their child. This is the case of "parentified children" – where the roles are reversed. The child becomes more concerned about their parent's well-being than their own. To acknowledge that their parents are not meeting their basic needs, or worse, that their parents are abusing them is too much for the child to face. Children deeply desire parental love and will seek it at any cost. Living in the stage of Denial and accepting their reality as normal is the path of least resistance. Often this is the only path available to a child growing up in challenging situations.

Once these individuals embark on a path of transformation the next stage they will need to enter into is Anger. Here they will become painfully aware of the pain they buried during their childhood. Unfortunately, many individuals never become free of this type of anger because they do not fully recognize the root source of their anger – unfulfilled parental love. Of course, even if our earthly parents cannot fulfill theses needs God can – and will. I am a firm believer that our parents couldn't have parented us differently given the wounds they carried. Allowing God into the space where the pain exists allows us to set a new course for ourselves, our children, and the generations that follow.

I have worked with many adults over the years with "anger issues" who were parentified children in their childhood. They tried, or are still trying, to "parent" their parents in an attempt to be loved and cared for. After all, only parents can provide a home, food, heat, and mother and father love for a child. A child is powerless to supply these needs on their own and they need to turn to their parents or other adults to supply these needs.

In these cases, the parents, for whatever reason, were unable to properly parent their child. When this happens we see a range of dynamics occur. From not being able to express love to their child, to not being able to meet their child's needs for food, clothing, and protection, or worse, to neglect and abuse, love is thwarted or vacant all together in the parent/child relationship. This was undoubtedly a result of the Fall that led to transgenerational entanglements as we have previously discussed. After all, our parents can only give what they received. The child then tried his or

AΩ 78 UNDERSTANDING THE JESUS CODE

her best to parent themselves. However, the child is just a child, and given this, is equipped with the skill sets and life experiences of a child. Children are ill-equipped to take on the job of a parent. This dynamic often sets an individual up to accept false beliefs about themselves and eventual failure.

While I did not personally suffer physical abuse in my childhood, I did witness recurrent physical and verbal abuse up until my parent's divorce when I was twelve. Memories of running and hiding under my bed still linger, yet, what is most poignant is the numbness I felt while the abuse was going on in my home – along with a wish that my father would leave the family. At some point during my early developmental years I learned that I needed to numb myself from the pain. My concern for my mother and younger siblings' well-being occupied my heart. I now see that I was a parentified child - fortunately I found God's healing love...

THE PAINFUL REALITY

There are two primary false beliefs I see in adults who were parentified children. The first false belief, and most damaging in my opinion, is a belief that they have to carry the weight of the world on their shoulders all alone. Often these individuals find it extremely difficult, if not impossible, to ask for help, especially those who identify with Enneagram type Three. Type Three individuals hold a core believe they need to achieve and perform in order to be loved. Asking for help can be experienced as a sense of failure or weakness that is internalized as shame. Deep-seated and misdirected independence is understandable when experienced by adults who were parentified children (regardless of your Enneagram type), because, after all, at a very young age these individuals needed to make many life decisions without proper guidance and direction. They often had to "go it alone" and this belief pattern became deeply imprinted in their subconscious mind. Patterns like these frequently lead many to mistrust individuals who have some sort of authority over them, even individuals who can offer real help such as teachers, coaches, and therapists. Of course I am not suggesting that it is good to blindly trust all in authority over us; however, the ability to discern who has your best interest at heart is clouded for individuals who have experienced life as a parentified child.

The second false belief I see these individuals possess is a belief that they are not good enough, or smart enough, and that they can't make good decisions. Remember, as a child they had to make many decisions that were beyond their ability and knowledge to make. Given this, they were set up for failure many times over. Inevitably, some of their decisions ended up causing them, or someone they loved, pain and heartache. This set of belief patterns will often hold an individual back from seeking care and guidance from others, including God. All of this is a great lie the Evil One tells us. Our human strength is limited and, in order to step into the fullness of life God offers, we must find our strength in him and not ourselves.

> Our human strength is limited and, in order to step into the fullness of life God offers, you must find your strength in him and not yourself.

Philippians 4:13 - I can do all things in him who strengthens me.

LIFE-LONG PATTERNS

Tough situations likely established belief patterns that will follow an individual throughout his or her life unless they engage in pattern interrupt of some kind. Belief patterns that led us to believe we are not worthy of love, no one will take care of us, we are a burden, or in order to survive we must take care of ourselves without the help of others not only do not serve us well, they are not congruent with God's plan for humanity. Often these belief patterns leaves us feeling inadequate, guilty, and shameful. None of this is true in the eyes of our communal God. In the eyes of God, we are worthy of love, there are people in the world who will take care of us, we are all wanted, and given that God created all of us to live in community, our survival depends on the support of others.

If you hold any of these beliefs then perhaps you grew up way too fast, and subsequently, you missed out on a significant part of your childhood. This form of role reversal, where you met the unfulfilled emotional and physical needs of your parents (and possibly other siblings), is often passed down through the generations. Like all pain, including transgenerational pain, the pattern can be reversed and a life lived fully alive can be realized. Such a life begins with accepting your parents for who they were, including the pain that stopped or blunted their ability to fully love and care for you.

If you were a parentified child, then it is likely that you frequently experienced pain you had to bury during your childhood. This pain was likely often the result of unrequited parent love, abuse, or neglect. You desired your parent's love, yet you knew it was somehow unavailable. This left you believing you had little or no foundational support to lean against in the world, and sadly, this is a reality for many children today. These children often feel alone in the world, and they frequently experience difficulty trusting others. All too often, repeated patterns like this leave individuals in a stage of Denial. And when these individuals become parents, well, they are numb and unavailable to give their children the love they seek from them. Sadly, the pattern continues until it is interrupted.

> *Matthew 18:10 - "See that you do not despise one of these little ones; for I tell you that in heaven their angels always behold the face of my Father who is in heaven."*

THE JESUS CODE CONNECTION
Hidden Wounds – Promise of New Life

BURIED PAIN TURNED INTO ANGER

As we discussed earlier, buried emotions cannot stay buried without a cost. Your body will need to process experienced pain in some way. There are two ways this can be accomplished. You can either develop a physical disease where the pain stays buried in your body and manifests as a physical ailment, or you can process the emotions through The Seven Stages of Healing. While the decision to choose to move through The Stages of Healing or surrender to a disease are, in part, made unconsciously, they are decisions you have some control over. Ultimately you will need to address buried emotions and move through the Stages of Healing if you desire real happiness.

A decision to fully surrender to God will lead to ultimate happiness and peace regardless of the path followed. This is true because your soul and God desire the same thing – oneness with God. This oneness is realized through the Second Person of the Holy Trinity, Jesus Christ. While moving through The Stage of Healing Anger will follow Denial. Your Triune God, with his perfect love and compassion, is with you every step of the way.

> *John 17:22-23 – "The glory that you have given me*
> *I have given them, so that they may be one, as we*
> *are one, I in them and you in me, that they may*
> *become completely one, so that the world may*
> *know that you have sent me and have loved them*
> *even as you have loved me."*

THE ENNEAGRAM TRIADS AND THE ANGER RESPONSE

Erupting bouts of anger may appear as you attempt healing and transformation. While all Enneagram types experience anger, those in the Body Triad; types Eight, Nine, and One, own it in a particular way. Here I will offer brief insight into this triad.

Type Eight individuals are self-confident and dominating. They are natural leaders who are decisive and straight-talking. While they can sometimes appear to be a grizzly bear on the outside, under their tough exterior lives a gentle and very loving teddy bear who not only wants to be loved, he or she deeply desires to take care of those needing protection. This is especially true for their family members. They experience exceptional heartfelt tenderness for the oppressed and marginalized in the world. Internally they experience a bit of God's magnanimous power. Donald Trump and Saint Mother Teresa of Calcutta are both examples of Type Eight individuals. However, when Type Eight individuals are stuck in their buried wounds they will express revenge in a big way. Then their behavior can be very volatile and explosive. Revenge is their particular flavor of anger. I'll get you before you get me tends to be their motto. This motto makes their defense looks like offense to everyone else.

Individuals who identify with Type Nine are easy going and agreeable people. They are optimistic and supportive of others. Think peace here. These individuals seek a conflict free world and they are very good at bringing people together. Several American presidents are examples of Type Nine individuals. Abraham Lincoln, Gerald Ford, Ronald Reagan, George W. Bush, John F. Kennedy, and Barak Obama are all examples. They want everything to run smoothly. When the risk of losing peace becomes too heavy to bear they can fall into complacency and inertia. Like a stubborn ostrich, they can bury their head in the sand when the world becomes too chaotic and stressful. When this happens their anger moves inward. However, they cannot contain their anger inside forever. It must move back outward again. When Type Nine individuals are trapped in their internal wounds they find themselves trapped in passive – aggressive patterns with their anger. They are conflicted, they want to keep the peace so they bury their anger, yet, anger cannot be buried forever. It must come out and express itself at some point.

Type One individuals are principled and they strive for perfection. They are self-controlled, hard-working people with a strong sense of right and wrong. Always seeking to make the world a better place, they have high standards for themselves and others. Pope John Paul II and Jimmy Carter are examples of Type One individuals. They carry a deep need to be good people full of integrity. When events occur in their life that challenge this need they fall into frustration, which is their particular flavor of anger. Their frustration resembles buried internal spheres that are always trying to rise and escape. Type One individuals, when trapped in their wounds, find themselves playing a juggling act with these spheres. They constantly try to hide their spheres of frustration from the outside world in an attempt to not appear bad or defective to others.

Like a pressure cooker blowing off steam, you will need to release the steam at some point – regardless of your Enneagram type. When this happens, you are often blamed for your "bad" behavior and singled out as the bad guy (or girl), and the cycle of shame continues. This pattern will likely continue unless the pattern is interrupted with the truth Jesus offers.

As I mentioned, in Anger, you are aware there is a problem. You feel the pain, you feel the anger, the frustration, the resentment, the passive-aggression, and that someone else is to blame. Instead of turning to God, you are tempted to direct your fury toward another, toward the one(s) who have harmed you or the one who you feel safest to vent toward. Justice must be done; however, you are trapped because no amount of justice will heal the pain. Only forgiveness can bring relief; however, forgiveness can be hard when the pain is profound. You can surrender this pain at the foot of the cross, give it to Jesus, ask for his love and forgiveness for yourself and your family. He can bring needed healing into your heart so that you can experience the freedom of God's love.

> *Ephesians 4:31-32 - Put away from you all*
> *bitterness and wrath and anger and wrangling and*
> *slander, together with all malice, and be kind to*
> *one another, tenderhearted, forgiving one another,*
> *as God in Christ has forgiven you.*

STAGE 3: BARGAINING

In Denial, we do not realize that God's mercy and love are freely given, in Anger we desire justice, and in Bargaining, we place our

> In Denial, we do not realize that God's mercy and love are freely given, in Anger we desire justice, and in Bargaining, we place our hope outside of ourselves.

hope outside of ourselves. What we miss in all three stages is the fact that there is nothing we need to do to deserve or receive God's love and mercy. God gives this to us freely. Once received, we will effortlessly place all our hope in God and allow his justice into our hearts. Yet we must take action and do God's will in order to benefit from these gifts to the fullest. These steps will include finding our way toward wholeness and life through healing our wounds. This type of true healing requires that we take ownership of our life and our pain. Jesus Christ will help us grow in forgiveness and acceptance every step of the way – we are never alone.

Psalm 94:19 - When the cares of my heart are many, thy consolations cheer my soul.

Bargaining, the third stage, can be called "let's make a deal." In Bargaining, you "know" you can experience happiness, wholeness, and peace; however, a *deal* has to be made. Either someone or something else in your life needs to change, or you believe that you need to change before happiness and peace can be experienced. Perhaps you believe your spouse needs to change, your parents need to change, your children need to change, your in-laws need to change, your boss needs to change, your friend needs to change, or the corporate/political/religious world needs to change before you can be happy. Or perhaps you need to do something to prove your worthiness; maybe you need to lose weight, finish a degree, or get a job promotion before you can be happy. All lies

> In Bargaining, you "know" you can experience happiness, wholeness, and peace; however, a deal has to be made.

propagated by the Evil One. When these patterns occur, you could go through your entire lifetime waiting for happiness to appear, only to find at the end of your life that it never showed up. Happiness is indeed and inside job, and always remember who dwells within your heart.

Bargaining can happen in the natural-healing world as well. When you believe that natural remedies and a healthy lifestyle are the Golden Ticket to happiness and peace, you are looking outside yourself for happiness. I have seen too many individuals come to me for help, carrying anger toward their medical doctor because this person didn't cure them. I then became the next practitioner in line who needed to fix them, and they wanted me to do it with natural remedies. However, in these cases, it is often not the natural remedies that are needed. Heart healing must come first, the natural remedies come second. The truth is, you can experience happiness and peace regardless of your physical health, and many a saint has demonstrated this over the centuries.

Remember, when you believe that someone or something outside of you must change before you can reach happiness, you are looking outside yourself for respite, when all the while the author of respite, Jesus Christ, lives inside of you. Surrender to him and give him your pain so you can fully live. As you grow in your trust of him, your faith will increase, and you will find yourself becoming an empty vessel. As you empty yourself, Christ will then enter in and fill you with his perfect love. Then you will find all the respite you could ever need within yourself.

> *Galatians 2:20 - "I have been crucified with Christ; it is no longer I who live, but Christ who lives in me; and the life I now live in the flesh I live by faith in the Son of God, who loved me and gave himself for me."*

THE JESUS CODE CONNECTION
True Healer – Jesus Within

MY PERSONAL BARGAIN

When I was a little girl my dad carried a fair bit of anger inside his heart. I am pretty sure he was an Enneagram Eight with a lot of buried wounds. Being a child I wanted his love, something he was unable to express for many reasons. I held onto the belief that if he could love me and not be angry I could be happy. Eventually my bargain changed and I came to believed that if he left I could be happy. Of course, neither was not true in the eyes of God. God knew I could be happy even if my dad couldn't show me the love I wanted. God also knew my father's pain and his buried wounds.

This desire for my father's love led me to pursue and obtain an undergraduate degree in mathematics as a young woman. Not inherently a bad thing—the world needs mathematicians. However, I studied math in an attempt to receive love from my father. My dad was a brilliant engineer and he was esteemed for his analytical mathematical mind. Since it was not my heart's desire to study mathematics (my heart simply wanted my father's love), my studies actually limited my ability to follow the voice of God. As I studied math I remember longing to study chemistry and biology, a longing I did not allow myself to indulge in.

Interestingly enough though – I did take a course on Christianity and another one on Buddhism while working on my undergraduate studies at Central Michigan University. Also, I remember with great fondness a math study group I participated in that was facilitated by a Catholic Nun while I was a student at Aquinas College in Grand Rapids Michigan. She was awesome and I thoroughly enjoyed sitting with her and chatting about all things math! God's voice still entered into my heart, even when my ears were muffled.

FALSE IDOLS AND BARGAIN

Bargaining can set you up to idolize something other than God, something you can wrongly follow in an attempt to be happy. My false god was "father love," and I sought it above listening to the voice of Father God. I believed that if I studied mathematics, I would receive all the father love my heart could ever desire from my dad.

The truth is, I could be happy with my dad just the way he was because he was the right dad for me. Through his wounds, and mine, I have learned how to love individuals who carry wounds like my dad's. My ability to love has expanded as a result of our relationship. I may not have experienced this increased ability to love had I had a different earthly father.

> Bargaining can set you up to idolize something other than God, which you can wrongly follow in an attempt to be happy.

Many of God's children have fallen victim to false bargains, and their God-given gifts have been thwarted as a result. It's not that seeking such endeavors is inherently wrong. It is the underlying belief that they are a prerequisite for happiness that causes the false idolization. True happiness can only be found in God.

COMMON BARGINS THAT LEAD TO FALSE IDOLS

Now let's look at a few common Bargains I have witnessed over my years in my practice and the false idolizations that often accompany them.

Common Bargain: When I get into this particular college, I can then be happy

False Idolization: Education.

Common Bargain: When my child gets into college, I can then be happy.

False Idolization: Your child's success.

Common Bargain: If I become an MD (pick any field), then I can be happy.

False Idolization: Worldly prestige, worldly love.

Common Bargain: If I become a mathematician, then I can be happy.

False Idolization: My father's love (wait this was mine!)

Common Bargain: If I take all these vitamins, then I can be healthy and happy.

False Idolization: Physical health through natural medicine.

Common Bargain: When I lose weight, I can then be happy.

False Idolization: Physical appearance.

Common Bargain: When I get through this part of my life, I can then be happy.

False Idolization: The future.

Common Bargain: When I get this new car, house, job, etc. I can then be happy.

False Idolization: A life different than the one you have.

Common Bargain: When my spouse (parent, child) changes then I can be happy.

False Idolization: A "perfect" life.

Common Bargain: When I am debt free, I can then be happy.

False Idolization: Money, financial stability.

What bargains in your life have connected you with false idolizations?

> *Matthew 6:33 - "But seek first his kingdom and his righteousness, and all these things shall be yours as well."*

THE JESUS CODE CONNECTION
True Promise – Peace of Mind

STAGE 4: DEPRESSION

In Depression, you feel as if all hope is gone and sadness often overcomes you. You will feel heavy, trapped, and like many, believe you are at your lowest point. I understand this phase rather well. I have experienced recurrent periods of depression in my life and I still carry a tendency to fall into this stage during periods of heartache – especially heartache where my children are concerned. However, I now recognize this about myself and when the cloud of sadness hovers around me I create extra space in my life to spend time alone with God. Also, if needed, I support myself with specific natural remedies to help lift my sadness.

The truth about this phase may surprise you. While in the stage of Depression you are very close to experiencing peace. Let me explain. In Depression, you once believed in a dream, and now that dream is not to be—a dream that often involved some change outside of yourself and involved a bargain of some kind. (If my children could be happy then I can be happy...). You needed *someone* or *something* to change. Now it is obvious that this change either may never happen, or it is completely outside of your hands.

"Danielle"

Several years ago I was working with a client I will call Danielle. Danielle came to me as most clients did back then: she was seeking help balancing her hormones naturally. As we continued to work together, it became clear to me that Danielle's real issue was rooted within her relationship with her belittling and narcissistic husband. He constantly made Danielle feel as if she wasn't good enough, she wasn't smart enough, she wasn't pretty enough, she wasn't a good mother, and she simply wasn't a desirable wife. None of this was true. Danielle was beautiful, funny, bright, she took leadership roles in many of the parent groups at her children's schools, and all four of her children not only excelled academically (one even gained entry into an Ivy-League university), but they were also a pure joy to be around.

As Danielle and I worked together, we knew that in order for her to find health and happiness, she needed to forgive her husband for his constant belittling and hurtful words. Additionally, she needed to find a way to love him as he is. Understandably, she held a lot of anger and resentment toward him, yet she deeply desired to save her marriage. Her pent-up emotions were affecting her physical, emotional, and spiritual health markedly. It became painfully clear that Danielle's husband would never seek the help he needed and his verbal abuse would continue indefinitely, unabated.

Danielle's anxiety was not subsiding at any noteworthy rate, and this prompted me to encourage Danielle to seek medical care from a psychiatrist. This resulted in medication and some respite. However, Danielle continued to experience anxiety, insomnia, and a host of other health-related concerns as a result of the marital stress. Eventually, Danielle sought the help of a pastor who would eventually guide her through the process of divorce. This was heartbreaking for all involved. However, Danielle is not called, nor anyone else for that matter, to remain in an abusive relationship.

Danielle's pastor helped her to see that. Sometimes we must walk away from an abuser, and this is what Danielle needed to do.

As Danielle moved away from her marriage, she transitioned from Bargaining to Depression. She had held hope that her husband would change for many years (Bargaining), and she did everything possible to support this change. Yet in the end, her husband chose to remain as he was. Now Danielle needed to face the reality of her life. She never wanted a divorce, and yet she was now a divorced single mother of four teenagers. My heart broke for Danielle as I watched her experience the sadness of depression. However, through it all, her relationship with Christ was strengthened because she continually sought respite in him during her trials. Danielle did eventually find peace and happiness.

SOUND FAMILIAR? HERE'S WHAT I DO

Have you ever experienced a tough walk in your life where you needed respite like Danielle? If so, I understand. Not only have I walked side by side with many clients during their struggles, but I too continue to experience my own struggles. When I find myself in the middle of a struggle there is something I do that has a huge impact on my emotional well-being. I go to a place of peace where I experience transformation and healing of my heart: the perpetual adoration chapel at my home parish. I invite you to do a quick Google search on the topic. In a nutshell, the Eucharist (the physical body of Jesus Christ) is exposed, and silence is observed. Individuals come to pray, meditate, and spend time with Jesus in this very unique way. What Jesus does to my heart in this chapel is beautiful and otherworldly.

Now mind you, if I am feeling depressed, I want nothing more than to crawl up in a little ball and hide from the world. If I am angry I would rather hold on to my anger and walk around the house seething. Yet I know it is up to me to make a change and transform my life. After all, I have been given the gift of free will, just like you.

We can choose to hold on to our pain, or we can choose to find a way to let it go.

If you find yourself in the stage of Depression, know that you can find peace when you turn your heart toward God. You can pray for escape and respite. You can pray and ask God to come into your heart and rescue you. Make no mistake, God hears every word. Unfortunately, if you do not know that perfect healing is available to you through Jesus Christ, you will not know where to turn to in your time of need. Instead of turning to God, you may turn to poor substitutes that lead to addictions—false idols that will steal your happiness, peace, hope, joy, and love. You see, depression stands at the gateway to happiness. The Evil One does not want you to know how close you are to what you seek. You will either persevere onward into Acceptance, or you will fall back into Bargaining, Anger, or Denial if you do not take the steps necessary to move toward God.

Psalm 34:18 - The Lord is near to the brokenhearted, and saves the crushed in spirit.

THE JESUS CODE CONNECTION
Almost Home – Peace Awaits

STAGE 5: ACCEPTANCE

What most individuals suffering from Depression don't realize is that they are very close to experiencing the peace of Acceptance! However, there seems to be a very thick, dark veil that needs to be annihilated and broken through before you can enter into the stage of Acceptance, a veil you

God will carry you across the veil through Jesus Christ and in the Holy Spirit.

do not need to dissolve or break on your own. As a matter of fact, you cannot dissolve and break this veil without the help of God. God will carry you across the veil through Jesus Christ and in the Holy Spirit. However, you must choose to resist the old patterns that have held you hostage. You must resist the trappings of sin that are ever present, trying to hold you captive under its ugly veil.

> Genesis 4:7 - If you do well, will you not be
> accepted? And if you do not do well, sin is couching
> at the door; its desire is for you, but you must
> master it.

THE JESUS CODE CONNECTION
Surrender – Perseverance

THE BEAUTY OF ACCEPTANCE

So what does Acceptance look and feel like, and how can you get there? To begin, let's briefly examine the similarities between Acceptance and Bargaining because to the untrained eye these two stages present themselves in very similar ways. Remember, when you are in Bargaining, you have hope, hope in a dream that you believe will bring happiness, and this can certainly put a spring in your step. In this stage, you engage in behavior that supports your dream, and often this behavior is a collection of positive actions.

Remember Danielle? When she was in Bargaining, she prayed for her husband, she was kind to him, she kept forgiving him, and she even began attending frequent daily Mass. These were all positive, life-giving behaviors that are congruent with happiness. However, through all of this, Danielle hoped in a dream that was outside of herself. She hoped that her husband would change and that this change would lead to her happiness. You see, happiness is never "out there." Happiness is to be found within you because you are a temple created for the Holy Spirit, and this Spirit wants to dwell within you.

1 Corinthians 6:19 - Do you not know that your
body is a temple of the Holy Spirit within you,
which you have from God? You are not your own.

Acceptance and Bargaining part ways inside your heart. With Acceptance, your heart is at peace. You no longer seek love and comfort outside of yourself, rather you turn inward to God. Yes, you still carry an awareness of pain and heartache, lost dreams, and disappointments. And your life can even look a bit (or a lot...) broken and out of control – from the outside. Yet, inside God's peace is growing. However, you have forgiven yourself and others and in doing so you experience a freedom that is not available in Bargaining.

With Acceptance, you are able to allow others the freedom to be who they are—even if they have hurt you. You are free to let them go if necessary, and you are free to allow them back if this is in alignment with God's design for your life. You begin placing all your trust in Christ, and even though you don't know what your journey will look like, you know that Jesus will lead you rightly. There is little turning back once you reach Acceptance. However, you must remain on guard and hold close to Christ during this stage, lest another trail come along and sweep you back into Denial, Anger, Bargaining, or Depression.

> With Acceptance, you are able to allow others the freedom to be who they are—even if they have hurt you.

Romans 15:13 - May the God of hope fill you with
all joy and peace in believing, so that by the power
of the Holy Spirit you may abound in hope.

THE JESUS CODE CONNECTION
Hope in New Life

STAGE 6: LOVE ENTERING IN

Once you have entered into Acceptance, you open your heart to receive greater love. You have looked at the painful parts of your life, you have released anger from your heart, you have forgiven others, you have begun to accept others where they are, and you are seeking Christ as your source of hope. Initially, Love Entering In is often experienced as a newfound lightness and peace of the heart. An inner happiness is beginning to dwell within, and others can see this when they look at you. Your heart is being healed as only the great physician, God himself, can heal it.

> Once you have entered into Acceptance, you open your heart to receive greater love.

ESCAPE FROM THE DARKNESS

Imagine for a moment a dark room, a room without windows and with a closed door. You are there alone, sitting on a chair, waiting for a little help so you can find your way out. Now see the door open a crack and a portion of gentle light enters in. With this new light, you can now see your way around the room a little. Now see the door open even more so that you can see what cleaning and repairs need to be done in this room. Maybe the room is full of dust bunnies and cobwebs and it needs a good spring cleaning. Maybe the room needs new paint, new furniture. Maybe you need to call in a professional to assist you with the repairs, or maybe the room needs a total overhaul because it was not built on solid ground. Heck, you may even look at the room and believe it needs a total overhaul beginning with a good bulldozer! Whatever the room needs, the light now enables you to see the next step because it has entered in and illuminated what was previously hidden. You can now see what needs to be healed in your life. Who you need to forgive, what aspects of your life you need to accept, and the pieces in your life that you need to release so you can love unconditionally like God loves all come into clearer vision.

Now imagine this dark room again. Except this time the room is full of your painful unresolved life experiences, experiences that need repair and healing. Some require a more complete awareness and understanding, some require forgiveness, some require the assistance of a specialist, and perhaps some are in need of a new foundation that will last. As the door opens, you can see what is going on a little better. Remember, the light is gentle and it will only reveal what your heart is ready to see. Peacefully, you develop an awareness of some of your painful life experiences that need transformation and healing. The power behind the gentle light has revealed what was hidden. Without it you would have remained captive in this dark room without any hope of transformation. The light gently enters in, ever so softly, and you are experiencing a newfound awareness of your life. A need to rely on Jesus for assistance arises from deep within your heart like never before. Now you realize that his gentle light has always been around you – offering comfort and care. Only now, you are free to let it in more fully.

> *Isaiah 58:8 -"Then your light shall break forth like the dawn, and your healing shall spring up quickly; your vindicator shall go before you, the glory of the Lord shall be your rear guard."*

As the door widens, more light and more comforting love enter. The more light that enters, the more you see the imperfections in your room, and the more you are compelled to take the steps necessary so that your room becomes your own personal oasis. You couldn't see those imperfections before; you couldn't see the cobwebs in the room, or the dust bunnies, or any of the dirt that is in the room. Now you can more clearly see the imperfections. Maybe you carry childhood wounds and betrayal, maybe you carry anger, maybe unforgiveness, maybe you pass judgment, and so the list goes. Whatever is in your room the healing light of Christ will heal it.

THE VIRGINS AND THEIR BRIDEGROOM

In an attempt to better understand how to connect with the healing power of Christ light let's look at the parable of the Ten Virgins and their Bridegroom.

At first blush this parable can appear counter Christian. After all, aren't called to share what we have with others? Especially when we need a little assistance finding God – our Bridegroom. Yes, as Christians we are indeed called to generosity and sharing. However, we can't share our personal love relationship with our Triune God any more than a lover can share their love with anyone other than their beloved. The love we share with another, especially God, is unique to each individual and it cannot be duplicated. This is the case with the wise virgins in this parable. The wise virgins had cultivated their love relationship with Christ and it was unique to each of them. Their deep bond with Christ opened the door into the glorious wedding feast. Their mature love relationship with him is symbolized by the oil in their lamps – I like to think of this oil as divine oil. It is perfect love.

Once oil is ignited it burns and a bright light comes forth. This light then allows us to see through the darkness. Without oil (or electricity...) we remain in darkness. The wise virgin's oil was burning bright for the Lord and it provided light in the darkness they faced in the world. The foolish virgins, on the other hand, didn't fully cultivate their love relationship with Christ and as a result they didn't have enough divine oil to see them through to the wedding feast.

Detachment

How can we become like the wise virgins – full of divine oil? We must grow in our ability to experience detachment – detachment from everything that separates our soul from complete union with God.

I believe that the wise virgins practiced detachment from the world. As a result of this detachment they arrived at a place of spiritual union with Christ. What does this mean for us today? Well, the world is full of things we can become easily attached to. From success to people to emotions, we live in a sea of distractions.

To become utterly detached from these distractions we must go to them, we must go to the merchants mentioned in this parable. In our relationship with our merchants we are presented opportunities to find divine oil. Our merchants come in many forms – all are unique to each individual. The merchants are the people we have relationships with. Sometimes we exchange love and the emotions congruent with love such as joy, peace, gratitude, and forgiveness. However, sometimes we exchange anger and the emotions congruent with anger such as fear, hate, jealousy, and unforgiveness.

Finding healing in our love relationships requires something of us – not our merchants (that would keep us stuck in Bargaining). We must choose to turn to our Triune God and ask him to help us become detached from what we think we need in our relationships with our merchants – even our need for love. Yes, even love as we understand it to be can limit our ability to receive divine oil. After all, God does not love like human beings love. His love is always bigger.

All too often human love is conditional or it comes at the price of heartache. God loves as only God can love – free of conditions and free from heartache. His love is still, constant, flowing, and infinite all at once. It is beyond time. His love is bigger than our human heart and mind can begin comprehend. Yet, this love is available to us – it can flow through us.

I believe Godly love is the divine oil the wise virgins carried in their lamps. In order to become full of this divine oil we must empty ourselves of all attachment to the world. In order to do this we can take a que from our early church fathers and mothers – we can go to the desert. Our early church fathers and mothers left the merchants and went into the desert to commune with God – just like Jesus did many times. I personally find my desert in the Adoration Chapel where I practice quite Contemplative Prayer.

So many people are hurting today. Our relationships with the merchants in our lives are strained – especially the merchants in our families. Our hearts are broken because our families are broken and hurting. Addictions, excluded family members, attacks on our families, and human heartache all separate us from peace. If you are hurting I invite you to sit in your desert and open yourself to the message God has for you through Contemplative Prayer. If you are looking for ways to pray then I invite you to visit a page on TheLIVEMethod.com titled: Fasting of the Mind. Allow yourself to become detached to the point that there is nothing of you in your relationship with your merchants – there is only God. Once this detachment happens you open a space for God to enter in and fill you with his Love – the perfect divine oil we seek.

THE JESUS CODE CONNECTION
Light – Life – Coming Home

TRANSFORMATION OF IMPERFECTIONS

As you start to look at these imperfections, you feel called into deeper prayer and meditation; you feel called to more fully understand what is going on. Your heart becomes filled with greater love, and your mind follows your heart's lead. All the effort you pour forth becomes effortless because it is no longer you leading the way, it is Christ. Now you have entered into the stage Love Entering In, the place where things begin to get easier. However, you have to go through the lower stages and do the work they require before you can get here.

Matthew 11:29-30 - "Take my yoke upon you, and learn from me; for I am gentle and lowly in heart, and you will find rest for your souls. For my yoke is easy, and my burden is light."

In the stage Love Entering In, the love God has for you enters into your heart in a beautiful, profound, and mystical way.

In the stage Love Entering In, the love God has for you enters into your heart in a beautiful, profound, and mystical way. Your heart begins to more fully receive the true tonic it needs in great doses. God's love abounds within you, and you then direct it toward your brothers and sisters. Through your trials, your heart has expanded, and you have learned how to beautifully love, forgive and accept others.

You once embraced the fragile innocence of childlike love, and you experienced hurt as a result, hurt that served to separate you from happiness and peace. Things have now changed. In this stage, you sustain a profound, beautiful, and enriched love for God that resembles the pure trust you held as a child. You now love God with childlike love, supported by the backbone of the trials and tribulations of your life. Your trust in love has come full circle. You have surrendered to Jesus Christ, and he has healed and transformed your heart. Now you are free to love him unabatedly without fear.

> You now love God with childlike love, supported by the backbone of the trials and tribulation of your life.

Matthew 19:14 - But Jesus said, "Let the little children come to me, and do not stop them; for it is to such as these that the kingdom of heaven belongs."

STAGE 7: LOVE CONSUMING

> *Matthew 16:24-26 - Then Jesus told his disciples, "If anyone would come after me, let him deny himself and take up his cross and follow me. For whoever would save his life will lose it, but whoever loses his life for my sake will find it. For what will it profit a man if he gains the whole world and forfeits his soul? Or what shall a man give in return for his soul?"*

Now it sounds as if the stage Love Entering In is the pinnacle of all possible transformation. After all, at that stage, your heart becomes filled with Christ's love, and you grow closer to God. You enjoy a greater love for others in the world, and you experience a sense of inner peace that only Jesus Christ can give. Basically, life is very good, and it would be easy to believe that you are living your life fully alive. However, are you really experiencing all that Jesus has to offer you? Can there be any more?

Admittedly, it is hard for me to see beyond Love Entering In because I have only received only a few small glimpses of the beauty that lies beyond it. Those fleeting moments when I am free to be them blame if someone else needs that, where I am detached from my own ego and pride so that another can heal. During those moments I feel God's love flowing through me, and then sadly, my ego steps in and tries to take control. I am still a work in progress...

However, a brief study of the lives of the saints and you are left with the knowledge that there exists a deeper, more profound love for our Lord. These men and women have given their all to Jesus for the sake of his kingdom. They sacrificed, they remained steadfast and singularly focused on Christ, they suffered all for the sake of his Name—some even to the point of painful death. They experienced a state of love that escapes me. They have picked up their cross and followed Jesus to the end, and in doing so, they have reached a state of perfection. Their lamps became full of divine oil through detachment.

TRUE SAINTS

So what does it look like when a saint follows Jesus and carries his or her cross? To begin, we must first grasp the true reason why Jesus carried his cross. He carried it so that we could live life fully alive. He *did not* carry it for the sake of the pain it promised. Carrying the cross was the pivotal piece required for our redemption. You see, when God's law is broken, when love is violated, a spiritual reversal must occur to bring about balance again. We see this in the Old Testament many times over when the Israelites offered sacrifice for the atonement of sins. Yet we are a new creation in Christ, no longer bound to the old law.

> When God's law is broken, when love is violated, a spiritual reversal must occur to bring about balance again.

Isaiah 53:5 - But he was wounded for our transgressions, crushed for our iniquities; upon him was the punishment that made us whole, and by his bruises we are healed.

Think for a moment how it feels when someone says or does something that hurts you. How do you feel afterward? Even though you did not initiate the harm, you feel the hurt. Now consider what it would take for you to feel better about the situation—aside from it never happening. Perhaps if your offender apologized and took some other action to make amends you could feel better? Maybe, maybe not—it depends on many factors doesn't it? Was the offense habitual, are they repeat offenders, was the action founded in malice, or was this an honest mistake? Then there is your piece in the entire ordeal: How good are you at extending forgiveness? How easy or difficult is it for you to trust again? What past memories come up and interfere with your offering of forgiveness?

Generally speaking, we are a people who bring forth more injury and harm in the world than love and forgiveness. Even when you deeply want to offer forgiveness, your baggage comes along for the ride doesn't it. All too often past memories and personal hang-ups limit your ability to heal from your wounds and experience peace with the one who has harmed you. Scales cover our eyes. Our scales impede our ability to see the world and our fellow brothers and sisters as God sees them. Our personal limitations then leave the door open for the Evil One to enter in. The next thing you know, you are falling away from love and forgiveness, back into anger, resentment and unforgiveness.

How can a reversal happen so that the entire world can move back toward God and his love? Because of our fallen nature, this is impossible for man. Remember Saul? His eyes were covered with scales. Scales from his life experiences that limited his ability to see clearly. His scales made it impossible for him to see goodness in the followers of Jesus. His scales led him to rampage against them – killing innocent men, women, and children. Scales of judgement, murder, hate, legalism, and so goes the list. However, God knew Saul's true heart and what he could become if the scales were removed. Before Saul could be used as God's chosen instrument Jesus needed to remove these scales. Once removed Saul became a new man. He became our beloved Paul, a man that lived, suffered and died for the Name.

Jesus can remove our scales too! Although it may not instantaneous like it was for Saul. After all, Saul was chosen for a very particular role in God's Kingdom wasn't he? Yet, God sent his only Son for all of mankind. It is he, the one without sin who is fully man and fully God, who alone has the power to transform sin and heal the pain it caused.

> *Romans 5:12, 21 Therefore as sin came into the world through one man and death through sin, and so death spread to all men because all men sinned . . . so that, as sin reigned in death, grace also might reign through righteousness to eternal life through Jesus Christ our Lord.*

THE JESUS CODE CONNECTION
The Triumph of the Cross

CARRYING YOUR CROSS

We know that Jesus carried the cross and endured its pain for us, for our healing and reunion with him. His pain had a purpose and that purpose was to draw us back to himself. Our individual pain is but a small portion of Christ' pain. And our individual crosses are but a small portion of his cross. Given this, our pain has a purpose – a sacred purpose. Through our pain we will move back to Jesus Christ and then back to the Father. This is all done in the milieu of the love of the Holy Spirit.

> *Hebrews 12:2-3 - Looking to Jesus the pioneer and perfecter of our faith, who for the joy that was set before him endured the cross, despising the shame, and is seated at the right hand of the throne of God.*

Your pain, your trials, and your challenging life experiences all present unique opportunities to move back to God. However, you must take the steps necessary so that your heart grows in love, forgiveness, and acceptance as a result of the trials. There is a saying that comes to mind here: "Become better, not bitter." These life experiences become the sum total of your cross only when you use them for their proper purpose—reunion with God. If they serve any other role in your life, you have missed a golden opportunity for happiness and peace. However, remember, due to our fallen nature, we will fall short of perfection (unless you become a saint—a worthy endeavor we should all try to achieve!). Given this, there will always be work to do.

We know that those who believe in Jesus share in his glory for the sole intention of unity with God. But what does it mean to share in Jesus's glory? This question begets another question, namely, what is Jesus's greatest glory? Triumph over sin and the salvation of the world—salvation for you and I! And how did his glory come to be?

He achieved victory over sin and death. How did he gain victory over sin and death? This is the story of the cross and all that comes with it —the painful and the joyful. Which leads me to my favorite scripture, John 17:22-23. (Yes, I did mention this scripture before – it is that special to me!)

> *John 17:22-23 - "The glory that you have given me I have given them, so that they may be one, as we are one, I in them and you in me, that they may become completely one, so that the world may know that you have sent me and have loved them even as you have loved me."*

God has given Jesus perfect glory and in turn, Jesus has given this perfect glory to us. That means we are called into perfection, a perfection we will only experience when we become one with Jesus Christ. Becoming one with Jesus demands that we become one with one another – just like Jesus is one with the Father. This is all accomplished so that the entire world will know that Jesus was sent by the Father, a Father who loves us as he loves his Son. When will we experience this? At the end of our transformational journey, a journey that can be experienced in this lifetime. Remember, Jesus told us that the Kingdom of Heaven is at hand. This means that God's Kingdom of love is available to us right now, right here. All we need to do is follow Jesus' way into the Kingdom. This journey is through our pain and buried wounds. On this journey we learn how forgive, accept, and love ourselves and others – seeing Christ in everyone we meet. Including the person in the mirror.

What does this type of love look like? The closest I can come to understanding this is by reflecting on the love I have for my children. Like most mothers, I would willingly sacrifice myself for them if I believed my sacrifice would take away their pain. Heck, I even sacrifice when it doesn't take away their pain! Yet my willingness to such sacrifice is conditional, isn't it? I could only give this type of sacrifice to my children, the ones who I carried within my body for nine months. Our saints are different and we can use them as role models. They sacrifice freely for others so that mankind can come to God through his son Jesus Christ.

Individuals who experience Love Consuming experience a Christ-like love for mankind that eludes most of us, a love that compels them to sacrifice freely for the sake of Jesus Christ. This love calls them to carry the weight of humanity in a very unique way—in a way that helps others carry what they cannot carry. They become so consumed with God's love that they can withstand any trial— even the trials of others. They can be the "victim soul" for others, they can be the martyr revealing a joyful countenance at the point of death, and they can live as a great saint. They have gone through the dark night of the soul, and they have experienced the painful separation from God that exists when one does not know him. They become equipped to carry the burden for others, through trials. Saint Mother Theresa of Calcutta, Saint Padre Pio, and countless other holy saints have reached Love Consuming. They became so consumed with love for Christ during their lives that this love called them to die to self so that others can live. By fully uniting their crosses with the cross of Christ, they became a perfected portion of Christ's body. They became a light for the world to see.

> *Matthew 5:15 - "Nor do men light a lamp and put it under a bushel, but on a stand, and it gives light to all in the house."*

THE JESUS CODE CONNECTION
Your Cross – Your Greatest Joy

WHAT STAGE ARE YOU AND YOUR LOVED ONES IN?

I invite you to ponder what Stage of Healing you and your loved ones are in. Regarding the different relationships in your life, what stage are you in? Perhaps with your children you are in Acceptance; however, with your spouse perhaps you are in Anger or Bargaining. What steps could you take to transform your heart and heal your family? How can you more positively impact the world with this knowledge and facilitate greater healing? I invite you to make notes in the blank pages at the end of this book.

« Chapter 7 »

The 3rd Face of Struggle: The Pain of Exclusion

Psalm 127:3-5 - Sons (daughters) are indeed a heritage from the Lord, the fruit of the womb a reward. Like arrows in the hand of a warrior are the sons (daughters) of one's youth. Happy is the man who has his quiver full of them. He shall not be put to shame when he speaks with his enemies in the gate.

Every human being has faced the pain of exclusion at one time or another in their lifetime, and undoubtedly, you have faced exclusion's piercing knife as well. Exclusion cuts profoundly deep into the depths of your body, heart, and soul because it is a violation of the law of God. By way of your creation, you were placed in a community, and in the eyes of God, you belong to this community. Just as the Father, Son, and Holy Spirit live a communal life, you too are created for community and inclusion.

As a human being, you were created by God to be dependent on others for survival, and without your family, you would not exist. Without your mother and your father, you would not even have the gift of life itself. You eat food that others have farmed, you drink water others have purified, you drive on roads others have paved, you wear clothes others have made, you live in homes others have built, and as a human being, you are dependent from your birth on your family for your survival for years (decades). Given this intrinsic interconnectedness of the human person, inclusion is part of our existence and to go against it leaves us wounded, with a sense of bitter isolation.

Exclusion from the family leaves a lasting painful imprint that can extend onward through generations, causing transgenerational entanglements that serve to place a burden on newer members of the family. Exclusion leaves children longing for their parents, parents longing for their children, siblings longing for one another, grandchildren longing for their grandparents, and it leaves both the excluded and the one excluding with a hole in their heart and soul. Fortunately, like all wounds, the wounds exclusion has placed within you do not have to forever separate you from happiness and peace. However, work must be done to bring about healing. In order to experience full happiness and peace, you must allow your heart to find resolution where the pain of exclusion has entered into your family. Perfect resolution can only be accomplished when you choose to follow Jesus Christ and allow yourself to be led by the Spirit.

THE JESUS CODE CONNECTION
Transform Exclusion – New Life – Inclusion

ADOPTED CHILD OF GOD

> *1 Corinthians 12:27 - Now you are the body of Christ and individually members of it.*

You are a member of the earthly family God placed you in; however, you are also part of something much bigger. Your heavenly Father has extended to you his tender care and you are his child. You are a cherished family member, a son or daughter of the one true King. You are a member of the Body of Christ – every human being is whether they realize it or not. We are all part of God's royal heavenly family. When any part of this sacred family is injured, the entire body feels the pain.

Yet it is not your responsibility to heal the entire Body of Christ all on your own. God calls you to heal the part of his Son's body that is uniquely yours—beginning with you and your earthly family. God desires that all families share with one another their burdens, offering strength and support—heavenly and earthly families alike. You are called to share your burdens with your brother Jesus in a very unique way—a life-giving way of truth. With the help of Jesus, you will find the healing balm that has the power to transform the wounds exclusion has left. He will suffer with you, he will carry you, and he will bring you into his full glory when you follow him with brotherly love.

> *Romans 8:14-17 - For all who are led by the Spirit of God are children of God. For you did not receive a spirit of slavery to fall back into fear, but you have received a spirit of adoption. When we cry, "Abba! Father!" it is that very Spirit bearing witness with our spirit that we are children of God, and if children, then heirs, heirs of God and joint heirs with Christ—if, in fact, we suffer with him so that we may also be glorified with him.*

THE #1 LOVE RULE

There are some basic rules surrounding the family that need to be honored in order for love to flow easily, and the #1 Love Rule lies at the foundation of the family. This is the rule of inclusion and it proclaims that everyone has a right to belong to the family they are born into. Inclusion, the #1 Love Rule, serves to facilitate happiness and peace in the family. Remember, God created and placed each and every one of us in the family we are born into, and with this knowledge, we can trust we are where we belong. When someone is excluded from the family unit, for whatever reason, the love God intended to flow is blunted and sometimes gravely thwarted. Once love is limited, heartache enters in, and the door to sin has been opened.

I know this can sound painfully excruciating to some, especially in cases of child abuse and abandonment. However, even in such heartbreaking cases, healing and transformation are possible with the help of the Holy Trinity. In order to believe that such pain is inescapable, you would have to believe that sin has greater power to destroy life than God's power to heal life itself. Of course this is not true. God, the creator of all life, has the power to heal all mankind's wounds.

> Psalm 146:3 - He heals the brokenhearted and
> binds up their wounds.

Remember, pain and heartache find their roots in sin. Someone, somewhere along the way submitted to sin, and the end result is pain and separation in the family. The road to wholeness will be strenuous and challenging for those who have suffered deep family wounds. It may be riddled with many setbacks along the way when extreme suffering has been experienced. But the journey will lead to a life of happiness and unimaginable peace when perseverance and trust in Christ win out.

> Romans 8:18 - I consider that the sufferings of this
> present time are not worth comparing with the
> glory about to be revealed to us.

THE JESUS CODE CONNECTION
Sin - Death

OUR COMMUNAL NATURE

We can look to the unity of the Holy Trinity for guidance when exploring the reality of our communal nature. Our God is a communal God: Father, Son, and Holy Spirit. Each part being fully whole and fully united with the other two. Looking to scripture, we see a significant number of passages revealing God's communal nature, and this could be a book all by itself. However, for this chapter, it is important to grasp that our God is communal and thus inclusionary in nature.

> *Genesis 1:26 - Then God said, "Let us make humankind in our image, according to our likeness."*

Beginning with Genesis, the first reference to God's communal nature is presented alongside the creation of mankind. The "us" and the "our" God is talking about is the Holy Trinity. This scripture passage, Genesis 1:26, in addition to revealing God's communal nature, reveals that mankind is made in his communal image and communal likeness. The unique creation of man sets mankind apart from all other creations of God. In no other scripture do we read that another creature is created in God's image. As God is communal, so is mankind—the only creature created in his image.

Then God, after creating them male and female, gave his creation a great gift—his blessing. He blessed the first man and woman before giving any further instruction, and this is significant. While he did say that his entire creation, the whole of the earth, was very good, he did not bless the rest of creation. He only blessed those he created in his communal image. After the blessing, God gave them instruction to go forth and multiply and subdue the earth.

> *Genesis 1:27-28 - So God created humankind in his image, in the image of God he created them; male and female he created them. God blessed them, and God said to them, "Be fruitful and multiply, and fill the earth and subdue it."*

From the beginning, God created the family to be held together, with its members supporting and caring for each other. Exclusion blocks the flow of love God intends for the family, leaving scars in the heart and soul of the one excluded, the one who excludes, and all who love them both. Exclusion leaves family members vulnerable to the outside world, without the safety net God offers.

> *1 Timothy 5:8 - And whoever does not provide for relatives, and especially for family members, has denied the faith and is worse than an unbeliever.*

THE JESUS CODE CONNECTION
In His Image – Truth- Communal

WHAT A CHILD CARRIES

Often a younger family member carries the greatest weight when someone is excluded. Let's explore this statement a bit. To begin, as a child, you come into this world ready to love and be loved in return. The smile on an infant's face as he interacts with his mother reveals this truth. However, you entered into a family where painful events occurred before your birth. You were helpless to heal this heartache because, after all, you were not part of its original impetus. Resolution needed to be found within the individuals where the hurt began. Love has been blunted many times before you came into your family, and this thwarting of love limits the full expression of love that God intends for all.

If you were born into a family where exclusion existed then you likely gave of yourself to heal the separation. Given the state of the world, you likely experienced the pain of exclusion at some level in your childhood. Sometimes families exclude their flesh and blood, while others exclude their earthly family members of different races, creeds, and cultures. As a child, you wanted to experience love in your family – your flesh and blood family as well as your earthly family. You would look on with confusion when it was withheld or absent. In an attempt to restore the flow of love, you sought to do the best thing you could do: you gave of yourself. The needs of your loved ones mattered more to you than your own needs. Additionally, your desire to be a part of this family mattered deeply, and you would sacrifice your happiness even if it cost you dearly.

Why such behavior? The answer can be found in your communal nature and your need to be a part of a family. God gave families glue to hold them together. This glue calls us to care for each other, especially the weakest and most vulnerable members of

> God gave families glue to hold them together... This glue is love.

our family. This glue is love. How could a baby survive without love? If our capacity to love one another was not part of our internal being then what would call a parent to give of him or herself to care for their vulnerable child? What would call us to tend to our vulnerable elderly, injured, or oppressed if not love? Without the glue of love the weakest would not survive and our species we would fail to exist.

Love needs to be restored when it is absent. Out of love you gave to your family—even to your detriment if you thought it necessary. You likely mourned the loss of your excluded family member, you lived with a broken heart, and it is probable that you sometimes exhibited depression or unexplained sadness. Or perhaps you chose to follow in the excluded one's footsteps, exhibiting similar behavior, as if in an attempt to give the family an opportunity to heal the root issue that led to the exclusion.

I now invite you to listen to the following scripture passage very slowly, with intention and focus. I know it is a passage you are familiar with; however, please hear it this time through the ears of a child who misses an excluded family member, a child who will endure all things for the sake of love.

> *1 Corinthians 13:4-7 - Love is patient; love is kind; love is not envious or boastful or arrogant or rude. It does not insist on its own way; it is not irritable or resentful; it does not rejoice in wrongdoing, but rejoices in the truth. It bears all things, believes all things, hopes all things, endures all things.*

> ## THE JESUS CODE CONNECTION
> *A Child's Love - Sacrifice*

BUT I HAVE MY REASONS

Perhaps you are saying to yourself that you have good reasons for excluding your parents from your children's lives, your ex-spouse, or troubled brother or sister, etc. I understand, bad things happen in this world and people make terrible decisions that cost not only themselves dearly, but also cost those who are in their family. However, remember, sin is found at the foundation of all pain in the world—including the pain in your family. The only antidote to sin is love. God's love holds the greatest power in the fabric of the world.

> Speak words of love and honor.

Love, especially the love of a child, will see the good and will seek to restore what God intends. My advice in circumstances of fractured love is this: Recognize that it is very likely that your child wants to love the excluded person (especially if the excluded person is their parent), and choose your words wisely. Work on taking yourself and your ego out of the picture. Speak words of love and honor. And remember, if you can't say anything nice, don't say anything at all. I have seen in numerous Family Constellations the profound sadness a client carries when a family member is excluded. Resolution has always been found when love is allowed to flow between the excluded person and the family.

You can be the safe harbor for your loved one when you open yourself to love. Of course this does not require that you open the door and allow the excluded person back in your life, as this is a complex area. However, you are called to love them where they are and to allow God to take it from there. As we saw with Danielle, sometimes you give the greatest gift when you walk away with love and forgiveness in your heart.

> *John 13:34-35 - "I give you a new commandment, that you love one another. Just as I have loved you, you also should love one another. By this everyone will know that you are my disciples, if you have love for one another."*

"Mark"

Mark was a twenty-six-year-old young man who came to me after suffering years of unexplained depression and an addiction to alcohol. Mark came from an upper middle-class family, and he experienced many privileges that come with such a life. His dad owned a successful business, and his mom was a stay-at-home mother. His family, while they claimed to be Lutheran, did not practice their faith outside of their Christmas and Easter service attendance. Mark had tried numerous prescription medications for his long-term depression, and he had sought the help of counseling for his addiction to alcoholism. He had experienced some relief; however, he still felt trapped and hopeless. Mark was willing to do anything to find respite, so I suggested a series of LIVE sessions. At first, he was a bit apprehensive, but he agreed, and we moved forward.

As we began his sessions, Mark shared with me the story of his older brother "Gary." Gary had gotten into the "wrong" crowd in middle school, and things escalated from there. Mark remembered shouting matches between his parents and Gary many times over. Mark shared with me that Gary was being disobedient to his parents, and he couldn't understand why. Eventually, Gary left home as a teenager, leaving Mark alone in the house with his parents. His mother became depressed, and his father poured himself into his work. This left Mark with a deep feeling of being alone in the world. Going deeper, Mark also shared that he was fearful of being disobedient to his parents, and given this, he became an obedient son. It turns out that Mark identified with

Enneagram type One and Gray identified with Enneagram type Eight. Mark earned good grades, he hung out with the "right kids," and he went to college. On the surface, Mark looked like he had it all together. After college graduation worked for a local pharmaceutical company and earned a nice income. He hid his alcoholism, and he didn't share with others that he took prescription drugs.

As we set up his Family Constellation in the office using figurines, Mark placed the figurines representing his parents in the center of the board and the figurine representing his brother a significant space away. Then it was time for Mark to place the figurine representing himself on the board. Mark couldn't do this, tears immediately filled his eyes and rolled down his cheeks. He proclaimed that he missed his brother and wanted to place his figurine near Gary; however, he couldn't leave his mother alone without a son, and he couldn't be disobedient to his parents. There it was. Mark wanted to be near his excluded brother, he felt responsible for his mother's happiness, and he placed his parent's wishes above his own happiness. Of course, being obedient to your parents and desiring your mother's happiness are not bad things; however, Mark sacrificed himself in an attempt to ensure these things. Above all, he wanted his brother back in the family. It was helpful for Mark to keep in mind that the issues between his parents and Gary didn't begin with him, and given this, Mark couldn't fix it. Mark believed that he was in an impossible situation.

I guided Mark through a series of LIVE statements that helped him find resolution over a course of five sessions. Today, Mark attends AA meetings, and he hasn't had a drink in one and a half years. He is off his prescription drugs, and he is following a healthy diet and lifestyle. He continues to see me as a naturopathic client. Most importantly, Mark now has a relationship with God. From this relationship, Mark was able to develop a relationship with Gary. Mark and Gary hang out together from time to time and Mark loves this time with his older brother. Gary and his parents have also developed a relationship, and while there is still work to do there, Mark has peace about it, and he doesn't feel the need to fix any of them.

SEEK AND FIND THE LOST

Matthew 18:12-14 - "If a man has a hundred sheep and one of them wanders away, what will he do? Won't he leave the ninety-nine others on the hills and go out to search for the one that is lost? And if he finds it, I tell you the truth, he will rejoice over it more than over the ninety-nine that didn't wander away! In the same way, it is not my heavenly Father's will that even one of these little ones should perish."

This parable almost doesn't make sense. Does risking ninety-nine for the sake of one lost sheep make sense? And an apparent wandering sheep at that? Does the lost sheep sound like Mark's brother Gary to you? This parable tells us that each and every one of us is valued and worthy of saving—even when the other sheep appear to take little or no notice of its absence.

Yet you are not a sheep. You are created in the image of the shepherd, and given this, when you suffer a loss of one of your fellow sheep, your hearts seeks to find it. Your soul yearns to be reunited with the lost one, and the lost one seeks to be reunited with you. However, a reunion is hard when sin has caused pain and separation. When you allow your heart to become numb and harden you cease to seek out the lost. When this happens you will lose out on the rejoicing a reunion promises.

> You are created in the image of the shepherd, and given this, when you suffer a loss of one of your fellow sheep, your hearts seeks to find it.

ORDER OF LOVE

Genesis 2:24 - Therefore a man leaves his father and his mother and clings to his wife, and they become one flesh.

God intended for love to flow in a particular order in a family, beginning with God extending love to the husband, who then extends it to his wife, who then extends it toward the children in order of their birth. Of course, the order of love could be another entire book. However, for this book, I will simply share with you the order of love. This will help you participate in the restoration of love in your family when exclusion has caused interruption.

Why does love begin with the husband? Why not the wife? Why not both simultaneously? Since both Creation stories of the Bible mention the man first, we can accept that the order of love begins with God, who then extends love to the man, who in turn extends love to his wife. In one Creation story Adam was in the dirt with God as they worked together, naming the animals of the earth together. God and Adam had a loving relationship before Eve was created. Then Eve came—the one who God created especially for Adam because he saw that it was not good for Adam to be alone. She was born in the garden—it's no wonder she was beautiful and Adam desired her so much. I will address more of the beautiful and symbiotic flow of love between man and woman in Chapter 10, "Father as Provider and Protector" and Chapter 13, "Mother as Nurture and Comforter."

THE JESUS CODE CONNECTION
Family – Foundation

ORDER OF PRECEDENCE

The relationship that comes first in a family takes precedence over the newer relationships. For example, mom and dad's relationship takes precedence over the mother-child and father-child relationships. With that being said, parents also carry a moral obligation and internal drive to love and protect their children. When both husband and wife love and respect each other as God intends, the children are loved and cared for. However, when there is heartache, the flow of love is compromised.

> *Proverbs 5:18-19 - Let your fountain be blessed,*
> *and rejoice in the wife of your youth, a lovely hind,*
> *a graceful doe. Let her affection fill you at all times*
> *with delight, be infatuated always with her love.*

There's a second component to the order of love that involves the creation of a new family. When a man marries, he leaves his family of origin to start a new family with his wife. This new family takes precedence, and his primary responsibility now lies in taking care of his wife and subsequent children. The same holds true for the wife, her primary responsibility now lies in caring for and loving her husband. However, both spouses are still tied to their family of origin, and given this, there are still moral obligations. The order of precedence has simply changed. This also holds true when a child is born into a family as a result of a second marriage. The new family, with a new child, take precedence over the previous family. This often causes significant heartache to children from a previous marriage. The Order of Precedence protects the youngest and most vulnerable in the family – the children.

> *Ephesians 5:31 - "For this reason a man shall leave*
> *his father and mother and be joined to his wife, and*
> *the two shall become one flesh."*

> *Ephesians 6:2 - "Honor your father and mother"—*
> *this is the first commandment with a promise.*

I understand that your family may not look traditional. Maybe you have a step-parent, step-siblings, half-siblings, and/or adopted siblings. Maybe you grew up in a single-parent home or you are the head of a single-parent home. Many of today's families do not mirror the "traditional family"; mine didn't. I understand the heartache that comes with such territory. It is important to grasp that all families today suffer pain, heartache, and a blunting of love. In order to live life fully alive these wounds must be addressed and healed. Broken families were not part of God's original plan, nor are they part of the dream a parent holds for their new born child. However, God can, and will, heal the pain of brokenness when we surrender to him.

THE JESUS CODE CONNECTION
Love – Family - Order

SELF-EXCLUSION

> *1 Corinthians 12:22, 25-27 - On the contrary, the parts of the body that seem to be weaker are indispensable . . . that there may be no division in the body, but that the members may have the same care for one another. If one member suffers, all suffer together; if one member is honored, all rejoice together.*

Individuals often exclude themselves from the family in one way or another. It is important to remember that any form of exclusion goes against God's law for the family, regardless of who initiated the exclusion. All members of the family are indispensable, and all are in need of care and community. Sometimes the care they need requires your prayers, or your expression of goodwill, or your forgiveness. No family member, at their core, wants to leave their family. One only leaves as the result of much pain and heartache.

> No family member, at their core, wants to leave their family. One only leaves as the result of much pain and heartache.

Pain of all kind can result in divorce, addictions, risky behavior, imprisonments, you name it. The list of exclusion catalysts is long and heartbreaking. The Evil One wants nothing more than to break up your family. Remember, the family sits at the foundation of society and the family is God's creation. If your family is suffering the pain of exclusion be ever mindful of who is at the source of such pain: Satan and his demons. It's time to take your family back and begin the healing process so you and the generations that follow will come to enjoy the inclusion and communal family love God offers his children. It's time to forgive one another and draw the lost back home. Your family can live a life fully alive. There is just a bit of work to do.

> Acts 2:39 - *"For the promise is for you, for your children, and for all who are far away, everyone whom the Lord our God calls to him."*

THE JESUS CODE CONNECTION
Family - Belong

« Chapter 8 »

The 4th Face of Struggle: Forgiveness of Self and Others

1 John 4:19 - We love because he first loved us.

Your soul craves forgiveness: forgiveness of self, forgiveness of others, and forgiveness of God. And for good reason. Through forgiveness real freedom is achieved. A freedom that promises to open the door to lasting happiness and peace. Without forgiveness, you remain trapped in a prison of harmful emotions. Yet, if you are like most individuals, you often find forgiveness an elusive and impossible dream.

> Your soul craves forgiveness: forgiveness of self, forgiveness of others, and forgiveness of God.

There are many reasons why forgiveness can be hard to experience; however, they can all be overcome with the right guidance. Forgiveness is a key component to The LIVE Method, and it is a key message in this book. All too often forgiveness is presented without the depth required for it to gain genuine entry into the human heart.

Too often a wounded heart is expected to forgive and forget too soon, before the soul has had the opportunity to allow for its full transformation. Too often humanity tends to confuse forgiveness with reconciliation, leaving the victim with a deep sense of guilt, shame, and powerlessness. Maybe this is you. If it is, then there is hope that forgiveness, true forgiveness, will provide a needed pathway for your soul's growth and ultimate happiness and peace.

> Forgiveness is beautiful, patient, multifaceted, mysterious, and healing, but most of all, forgiveness is a journey worth traveling and a journey your soul deeply yearns to experience.

When the need for forgiveness arises, you are presented with an opportunity to learn more about yourself and what you need to experience wholeness. While forgiveness may, at first blush, appear to be about the other person, it is actually a doorway into your own soul's journey and ultimate union with God. Forgiveness is beautiful, patient, multifaceted, mysterious, and healing, but most of all, forgiveness is a journey worth traveling and a journey your soul deeply yearns to experience.

FORGIVENESS OF SELF AND OTHERS – WHY FORGIVENESS?

We have learned up to this point that emotions have a significant impact on our physical health, our emotional health, and our spiritual health. We have also learned how detrimental exclusion can be in the family. Anger and unforgiveness are key emotions found in both topics, so let's take a look at them now. To begin, these two emotions separate your heart from experiencing the love God has for you. Additionally, anger and unforgiveness interfere with the growth of your spiritual gifts and their expression in the world.

We all know the feeling of anger; we've all been there. Given that love and anger are not congruent with each other, the times we have experienced anger are moments in our lives where love has been limited. Anger is often the result of unforgiveness, when someone has trespassed against you and when someone has wounded you. Both anger and unforgiveness hold power in your subconscious mind and both limit your ability to receive love.

JESUS AUTHORED FORGIVENESS

Jesus is the one who authored forgiveness for the world. We can look at some of his last words on the cross to see its importance. When you understand and recognize that when another harms you they truly do not know what they are doing then it becomes easier to forgive. I can hear you now. You may be saying, "Wait a minute. When Sally gossiped about me, she knew she hurt me. She knew what she was doing, and it's not right, it's not fair, and I'm hurt, and I'm angry." However, if Sally, within her heart, really understood the pain she inflicted on you, she could never have done the things she did. Because after all, we are all one body in Christ, and given this, when we harm another we also harm ourselves. Only hurt people, hurt others.

> *1 Corinthians 1:10 - Now I appeal to you, brothers and sisters, by the name of our Lord Jesus Christ, that all of you be in agreement and that there be no divisions among you, but that you be united in the same mind and the same purpose.*

You can look to the Lord's Prayer to further understand the importance forgiveness holds. In it, Jesus says, "Forgive us our trespasses as we forgive those who trespass against us." Many (most perhaps) Christians upon reading this line believe they are going to God asking for forgiveness in equal measure to their mere ability to forgive. If this is indeed the case, then it is as if we are saying to God - "God only forgive me as much as I forgive others who have hurt me." Yet, God always forgives in greater measure. Our humanity dictates that we cannot forgive to the measure that God forgives. If we ask God for forgiveness in equal measure to the forgiveness we extend towards others where does that leave us? In a dismal state I fear.

How could any human being ever forgive as much as God forgives? There is no way you could ever love as much as God loves and there is no way you could ever forgive as much as God forgives. I believe Jesus is giving a very literal interpretation here. He is instructing us to go to the Father and ask him to forgive our trespasses as we are forgiving those who trespass against us. Meaning, we are forgiving as best we can and we are trying to forgive others more fully all the time. We are trying to continually expand our ability to forgive. As we do this we grow in the grace of forgiveness. God then pours his forgiveness and mercy over us.

In the end, you will discover that as you grow in forgiveness, your heart will experience greater love, happiness, and peace. Because after all, with forgiveness, anger leaves, and love rushes into your heart. You must persevere and grow in forgiveness. In turn, God will heal your heart through Jesus Christ. Now the work begins.

The first question you may have at this point likely concerns the starting process. How do you start to forgive someone who has harmed you? How do you ascend out of painful anger and unforgiveness? A good first step is to pray for the person who has harmed you. Ask God to bless them, after all, you may be the only person praying for them. Jesus was very clear when he told us to pray for those who harm us. Prayer clears the space, and the energy, between the two of you. Instead of anger and unforgiveness hanging in the air, prayer permeates it. Then the Holy Trinity can come in and purify the space. During this type of transformation something beautiful happens to your heart, it begins to open and receive greater love.

Romans 12:14 - Bless those who persecute you; bless and do not curse them.

THE JESUS CODE CONNECTION
Forgiveness – True Power

WHAT FORGIVENESS IS AND WHAT IT IS NOT

To begin, forgiveness is a gift you give yourself. Forgiveness is not about the person who has hurt you, and it is not something you give to another. Yes, by extending forgiveness, the one who has harmed you will benefit in some way because they will receive forgiveness and love from you instead of unforgiveness and anger. This is God's will my friend. Isn't this exactly what Jesus called you to do when he told you to love your brother as yourself? By extending forgiveness, your heart becomes more Christ-like.

> Harboring unforgiveness takes a lot of energy—energy you could use in areas of your life that offer fulfillment and happiness.

Further, by embracing forgiveness, you must face your sinful part in the relationship—even if your only part is holding unforgiveness in your heart. Once you surrender to forgiveness you open yourself to God's mercy and aid. Harboring unforgiveness takes a lot of energy—energy you could use in areas of your life that offer fulfillment and happiness.

Psalm 51:3-4 - For I know my transgressions, and my sin is ever before me. Against thee, thee only, have I sinned, and done that which is evil in thy sight.

> Remember, forgiveness does not give another person permission to hurt you again.

Remember, forgiveness does not give another person permission to hurt you again. If someone is hurting you, then you become the victim, and they become the wrongdoer. In both cases, neither person is living a life fully alive as God intends. God doesn't want you to be a victim any more than he wants the other to be the wrongdoer. Sometimes the best thing we can do for the one who is harming us is to let them go, providing we walk away with love and forgiveness in our heart and pray that they find their way to Jesus Christ.

FORGIVENESS OF SELF

> *Isaiah 1:18 - "Come now, let us argue it out, says the Lord: though your sins are like scarlet, they shall be like snow; though they are red like crimson, they shall become like wool."*

Multitudes of God's children suffer because they can't forgive themselves for past behavior, often behavior that resulted from passed down family patterns and transgenerational entanglements. Subconscious files play over and over creating a life of limited abundance, happiness, and peace. Getting to the root of these patterns and turning them around is central to living fully alive. After all, how can you see the best in the world if you constantly employ negative self-talk? How can you enjoy relationships to the fullest if you believe you don't fit in or you are flawed in some way?

To break this down, let's examine two common limiting beliefs I have observed over the years with my clients. Limiting beliefs quell the expression of mankind's God-given gifts in the world.

1. Good guys finish last.

2. Rich people are evil.

Both are limiting beliefs, and both will hold you back from financial prosperity and abundance. If you believe that "Good guys finish last," then given that your heart is good, you will subconsciously align yourself with the last-finishing "good guy" because only the "bad guys" finish first. To believe that rich people are evil is the same thing. You won't allow yourself to experience financial abundance and prosperity because only "evil" people do that.

Let me ask you a question. If you were to experience a significant windfall in your financial portfolio today, what would you do with it? Would you give more to your church? Would you give more to charity? Would you start a foundation? Knowing my audience, I suspect you would do significant good with your windfall! As a matter of fact, my guess is that you have already dreamed of all the good you would do if you "had the money to do it."

Another set of limiting beliefs that I see creates havoc in families are as follows.

1. Men are bad.

2. Women can't be trusted.

If a man believes women can't be trusted, then what type of a woman is he going to be comfortable with? He will seek a woman who he believes he can't trust because that is what his subconscious mind if congruent with. Or, likewise, if a woman believes that all men are bad, what type of man will she seek out? You guessed it: a man she perceives as bad. In order to live the life of abundance, happiness, and peace, you have to rewrite limiting beliefs and turn them around so that they become the beliefs that are congruent with God's intentions for your life. Remember whose image you are created in.

THE JESUS CODE CONNECTION
Self-Love – Forgive

WE NEED A SAVIOR

I understand it sometimes feels hard, if not impossible, to forgive. This is why we need a savior. We need someone with the power to heal the transgressions that humanity has committed against itself. When someone transgresses against another, they take something unjustly from them. They take happiness, self-esteem, peace of mind, physical safety, and on the list goes. The transgressor steals something from the one transgressed against. Thievery is in the realm of Satan, the thief who has come to steal your joy. The only way to reverse transgressions is through the one who has defeated Satan, Jesus Christ.

While we may try to forgive, our fallen nature limits the power forgiveness offers us. Too often we allow anger to penetrate and weaken forgiveness. Our heart experiences forgiveness one moment, only to turn to anger the next. When we can't forgive in equal measure to the transgression, the spiritual scales are tipped toward the darkness found in the transgression.

THE DEBT OF TRANSGRESSIONS

Here is a little story to paint the picture for you. Let's say that a woman comes up to you and asks you for 5 dollars. She looks hungry, so you happily give her 5 dollars because you are a generous person. Then she asks for 10 dollars—her kids are hungry too. You are still feeling a bit generous, so you give her another 10 dollars. Then she asks for the 20 dollar bill she sees in your hand. At that point, you notice the smell of cigarettes and alcohol on her, and you politely tell her you can't give her 20 more dollars. Now you are beginning to regret giving her the 15 dollars you already gave her! She crossed a line and got greedy. She threatened to trespass against you and take something unjustly. You were good with the 15 dollars; however, 35 dollars crossed the line.

Before you know it, she snatches the 20 dollar bill out of your hands and runs away with the entire 35 dollars! Now how do you feel? Angry I assume. Then a bit of time passes and after a while you calm down; remember, you're a good Christian. Hopefully you have been able to calm down enough to forgive her for the first 15 dollars you gave her. But what about the 20 dollar bill she snatched out of your hands? If forgiveness does not counterbalance the spiritual effects of the transgression, a spiritual vacuum is created. If you can't forgive to balance this out, then who can? What if no one could ever balance out the spiritual vacuums transgressions create? Where would we be—spiritually speaking? In a very dark abyss.

You see, only a sinless Savior who is fully human and fully divine, one who has battled Satan and won can fully counter transgressions. Only a Savior such as this can balance out the stolen 35 dollars. Our sinless savior, Jesus Christ, through whom all forgiveness moves, is the one we must turn to when we need the grace of forgiveness in our lives.

> *Ephesians 1:7 - In him we have redemption*
> *through his blood, the forgiveness of our*
> *trespasses, according to the riches of his grace.*

THE JESUS CODE CONNECTION
Jesus Christ – Ultimate Transformer - Forgiveness

« Chapter 9 »

The 5th Face of Struggle: Overcoming Childhood Wounds

Saint Teresa of Avila - "Let nothing disturb thee; Let nothing dismay thee: All thing pass; God never changes. Patience attains all that it strives for. He who has God finds he lacks nothing: God alone suffices."

The experiences you encountered in your childhood have left lasting imprints in your body, heart, and soul that you will carry throughout your lifetime. Such imprints color how you see the world, how you interact with others, and how you see yourself. Your unique childhood experiences left you with the perspective of viewing the world that is uniquely yours. Perhaps you see the world as an exciting place where boundless happiness and peace is possible, or perhaps

> Your unique childhood experiences left you with the perspective of viewing the world that is uniquely yours.

you see the world and wonder what the point of it all is. More than likely your viewpoint of the world falls somewhere in between these two.

Whatever your childhood experiences have been, know that you can live fully alive. You can be that happy person that everyone wants to be around—you know, the man or woman who always seems to have a spring in his or her step and a smile on his or her face. And if you are that happy person, then you can learn how to take your joy to the next level so that you have an even greater positive impact on the world around you. Regardless of where you are on the "happy spectrum" your next step toward a fuller life begins by tackling the limiting beliefs you developed in your formative years. And unless you are a person who loves each and every individual on this earth (even the "bad" guys) 100 percent of the time, 24/7, then you have work to do if you want to experience all of the abundance, happiness, and peace God has for you. Remember, God intends a life of fullness for you and the generations that follow you.

In order to live a life full of happiness and peace, you must address the transgenerational entanglements that are the seeds of your limiting beliefs, and transform them. You do not need to carry forth the patterns in your family that are not congruent with God's plan for your life. Heck, these patterns were not God's plans for your ancestors either; however, your ancestors didn't know how to escape the madness back in the day! However, today is different. You have resources available that the previous generations didn't have. You have books, support groups, retreats, seminars, and bible study groups. A quick Google search and you will find what your heart needs.

> God made you a promise. When you turn toward him, nothing is beyond his repair—he can transform everything with his love.

God made you a promise. When you turn toward him, nothing is beyond his repair—he can transform everything with his love. No more do you need to live with the "guilt" of your parents, because God sent his Son to save the world. Yet you must take the steps necessary to develop a relationship with him and receive the healing that only he can give.

> *Jeremiah 32:17-19 - "Ah Lord God! It is you who made the heavens and the earth by your great power and by your outstretched arm! Nothing is too hard for you. You show steadfast love to the thousandth generation, but repay the guilt of parents into the laps of their children after them, O great and mighty God whose name is the Lord of hosts, great in counsel and mighty in deed; whose eyes are open to all the ways of mortals, rewarding all according to their ways and according to the fruit of their doings."*
>
> *John 3:17 - "For God sent the Son into the world, not to condemn the world, but that the world might be saved through him."*

THE JESUS CODE CONNECTION
Childhood Wounds – Springboard – New Life

THE IMPACT ON YOUR BRAIN

Your childhood experiences affected not only your emotional body, but they also affected how your brain neurons and synapses developed from the earliest moments of your existence. Modern science reveals that the human brain begins its development within the first few weeks after conception.

Your childhood experiences affected not only your emotional body, but they also affected how your brain neurons and synapses developed from the earliest moments of your existence.

The feelings your mother held toward your father and her pregnancy, and the feelings your father carried have all left an imprint on you. These early experiences play a part in the emotions and behaviors you experience to this very day—the good and the bad. They have become part of your subconscious mind. They are like tapes playing in the background of your mind, and they are calling the shots. These early experiences are your own unique internal programming. When the programming is not congruent with your soul's highest desires, you will experience pain in your life. However, this programming can be overwritten, and you can step into a new life, a life where you experience happiness and peace.

> Luke 18:27 - But he said, "What is impossible with men is possible with God."

Let's face it, earth is not for the weak-hearted. Every human being is destined to experience pain. As I often tell my children and grandchildren, be kind to others because you never know the hidden wounds they carry. Once you understand that everyone carries buried pain, including yourself, the question then becomes, how can you transform the buried pain in your life so you can experience true happiness and peace?

> Regardless of the level of intensity of your early childhood pain, your early experiences are the root cause of many limiting beliefs.

One of the first steps in understanding buried pain is to develop an understanding of the effect your childhood experiences had on you, especially your in-utero and early childhood experiences. Numerous studies have drawn a direct link between early childhood trauma and impaired physical and emotional health. Of course, not everyone has experienced early childhood trauma; however, each and every one of us has experienced heartache at some level in our early years—even if it is not getting the toy we want on Christmas! Regardless of the level of intensity of your early childhood pain, your early experiences are the root cause of many limiting beliefs. Sadly, all too often, individuals never break free from limiting beliefs and as a result end up living an incomplete life. This does not have to be the case. Real change is possible. You are God's child, and you were created to live a rich and full life.

> *Jeremiah 29:11-13 - For I know the plans I have for you, says the Lord, plans for welfare and not for evil, to give you a future and a hope. Then you will call upon me and come and pray to me, and I will hear you. You will seek me and find me; when you seek me with all your heart.*

IN-UTERO EXPEREINCES

Research indicates that the physical, emotional, and spiritual environment an unborn child experiences leaves lifelong marks on the child—for good and for bad. This is not surprising given that fact that you can be profoundly affected when a loved one is experiencing a strong emotion. When considering an unborn child's experiences, you must also take into consideration the intimate sharing of not only emotions but also biochemicals, including hormones that produce stress (or peace) between the child and his or her mother. In today's modern world, we see babies born into the world with stressed adrenal glands because mom was stressed beyond her capacity to adequately handle stress during the pregnancy. In light of this, it is helpful to understand that the best gift you can give an unborn child is a happy and healthy mother. However, society must change before this can happen on a large scale, and that change needs to be rooted in the one who alone can transform our hearts—Jesus Christ.

It is well documented that unborn babies experience a variety of experiences during their in-utero time. When the experiences are positive, the child looks at the world through the lens of goodness, hope, joy, and love. This is God's plan for each and every one of us. All of the unborn child's experiences create beliefs—both positive and limiting. Over my many years in practice I have found several significant in-utero experiences that lead to weighty limiting beliefs.

In-utero Experiences Found at the Core of Many Limiting Belief Patterns

- Conception out of wedlock, adultery, or conception in a drug-dependent relationship.

- A father's rejection toward the mother or the child.

- Physical or emotional abuse of the mother.

- Prior miscarriages or abortions of the mother.

- Being conceived at the "wrong time" (marital problems, poverty, etc.).

- Being the "wrong" sex.

- A mother who experiences intense emotions.

- A difficult birth.

- Adoption or considered adoption.

Each of these situations can set into motion a unique set of limiting beliefs in the developing child's subconscious mind. Given that studies reveal that 95% of our behavior stems from our subconscious mind, if you have experienced any of the above life circumstances then I invite you to find a way to transform them so you can experience all the happiness and peace God has for you. You may find LIVE Language, which is explored and outlined in Chapter 15, to be a useful transformational tool. You may also find the story that follows helpful. Remember, through Jesus all healing and transformation is possible.

THE JESUS CODE CONNECTION
Truth – God's Eyes – Beloved

"Sharon"

I will share with you the story of a client of mine I will call Sharon. Sharon was an attractive twenty-eight-year-old single mother of a three-year-old son, and a competent accountant when she came to see me for weight loss. It didn't take long before we started working on her emotional and spiritual transformation. Sharon was conceived out of wedlock, and even though her parents married, she never felt she belonged, no matter what group she was involved with. She was promiscuous as a teenager and young adult, and she always attracted men who would never stick around. It became clear to both of us during her session that being conceived out of wedlock made her feel she wasn't as good like the "good girls," and even worse, she believed she was inherently "bad."

Sharon also identified with Enneagram type One. Given this identification Sharon's belief that she was somehow not perfect cut deep and created profound internal frustration. Her subconscious voice constantly told her she was inherently flawed and sinful and she needed to continually seek perfection. On top of this, Sharon grew up in a rather religious home where there was a definitive line between right and wrong. You were either right and good, or you were, well, less than. A difficult environment for an Enneagram One individual regardless of their birth circumstances.

Sharon carried many limiting beliefs that separated her from fully living. She also carried shame, which was revealed in her false belief that she was inherently bad. If you have experienced life circumstances similar to Sharon then I invite you to determine if the following LIVE statements that Sharon repeated during her LIVE sessions would be of benefit to you.

Key Forgiveness Statements for Sharon

- I forgive myself for believing that children conceived out of wedlock are not worthy of love and they are not as good as a child conceived inside of wedlock.

- I forgive myself for believing that I have to carry this burden of infidelity in my body, heart, and soul.

- I forgive myself for believing I'm not as good as the "good" girls.

- I forgive myself for believing that I am not a good girl.

- I forgive myself for believing that I have to prove myself to be a good girl, before God and others can see me as a good girl.

- I forgive myself for believing that men only value me for my body.

- I forgive myself for believing that I have nothing of value to give a man other than my body.

- *Mom and Dad Statements*

- I leave with my mom and dad what is theirs to carry surrounding my conception, and I will carry what is mine to carry.

- I trust that God will help my parents move beyond their guilt and shame surrounding their decision to engage in pre-marital sex and their guilt is not mine to carry anymore.

Spiritual Freedom Statements

- I call up all the guilt and shame I have carried in my body, heart, and soul as the result of my being conceived out of wedlock and I lay it at the foot of the cross for Jesus to do with it as he wishes. I then ask that God, through Jesus and in the Holy Spirit come into that space, heal it, and turn it around so I can see the truth of my worth through God's eyes.

- I ask God to reformat my physical body, heart, and mind so they function in a way that is congruent with the life God intends for me to live, free of the weight of living under the deceitful veil of guilt and shame that has shrouded my conception.

- I proclaim in the name of Jesus that all emotions I have ever felt surrounding my conception only serve to bring me closer to God, Jesus, and the Holy Spirit.

THE JESUS CODE CONNECTION
Mon – Dad – Family Bonds

CHILDREN SACRIFICE FOR LOVE

> Given the innocence of a child's love, she willingly sacrifices a great deal of herself.

As discussed in the chapter on exclusion, children will sacrifice out of love if they believe their sacrifice can heal the family. In Sharon's case, she believed she had to carry the burden of being conceived out of wedlock for her parents, out of fear that their church would reject her parents if they knew the truth about her conception. In short, Sharon was trying her best to protect her parents from harm – she was sacrificing herself. A child will attempt to take on the pain of her loved one: her parents, her siblings, her grandparents, and even her aunts or uncles. We must keep in mind that a child's love is more innocent than an adult's love. She hasn't built up the many walls that hinder love, the walls humans create to protect themselves from the hurt of not being loved. Given the innocence of her child-like love, Sharon willingly sacrificed a great deal of herself for her parents.

However, a child, like Sharon, is set up for failure because the pain of her loved one is not her pain to heal; it is the loved one's pain to carry, transform, and heal. It is her loved one who needs to offer the forgiveness and acceptance necessary for the transformation of heart to occur. Both of Sharon's parents needed to do their own forgiveness work surrounding their premarital activity. Once the necessary forgiveness and acceptance occur the child then becomes free to love as her pure heart desires.

More than likely, the root source of pain occurred before a child was born into a family. In Sharon's case, her mother had been abused in her childhood. Her abuse led her to both devalue herself and allow pre-marital relations while she also searched for someone to love her. Often the pain is the result of generational hurts going back who knows how far—the root of hurts such as unforgiveness, shame, anger, betrayal, resentment, fear, and guilt extend back to the original sin of Adam and Eve. When we come to peace with those who came before us a space is created for healing to occur. Sharon had to come to peace with her conception and her family before she could see herself as a valued child of God.

> When we come to peace with those who came before us, a space is created for healing to occur.

Unfortunately, as a result of the failed attempt to heal her parent's pain Sharon took on false beliefs about herself. These beliefs led to promiscuity and unrequited love. Sharon could have passed these beliefs on to her son. Fortunately, she sought transformation and now her son will live a different life as a result. I am happy to say that Sharon is a happy woman today and she has had a steady boyfriend for almost a year! She now sees her self-worth and she has even taken up running.

Common Limiting Beliefs

I'll share with you some common limiting beliefs that I see in my clients. Limiting beliefs that tend to find their origin in childhood experiences. Maybe you will see yourself or a loved one here:

- I'm to blame.

- It's hopeless.

- I'm not good enough.

- I don't belong.

- I'm unloveable.

- I'll never be free of this pain.

- I can't love Mom without feeling her pain (same with Dad and siblings).

- I'm responsible for my mother's happiness, or my father's.

- If I take on their pain, they can heal, and then they will love me.

- I need to be broken to receive love.

- If they find out the truth about me, they won't love me.

- I can't be happy without his or her love.

- Men (or women) are not safe to be around.

- The world isn't safe.

- People are out to get me.

Are you beginning to see how your early experiences can limit your ability to fully live? In order to live fully alive, you must become free of the false and limiting beliefs that hold you back. I believe we are living in a unique time in history. A time where we are learning the truth, the truth that is the ticket to freedom and happiness. You are living in a time where you can finally turn this pain around so that along with your children and the generations that follow, you can experience a full life of joy. However, you must take the steps necessary for the transformation to occur.

Ephesians 4:13-15 - Until we all reach unity in faith and knowledge of the Son of God and form the perfect Man, fully mature with the fullness of Christ himself. Then we shall no longer be children, or tossed one way and another, and carried hither and thither by every new gust of teaching, at the mercy of all the tricks people play and their unscrupulousness in deliberate deception.

THE JESUS CODE CONNECTION
Limiting Beliefs – Transformation – Joy

« Chapter 10 »

The 6th Face of Struggle: Father as Provider and Protector

Thomas Merton - "The real reason why so few men believe in God is that they have ceased to believe that even a God can love them."

L ife under the protection and provision of a strong, loving father allows a child to grow within the ever-present security needed for happiness and peace. However, in today's world, many do not experience a childhood within a shielded sanctuary. Our earthly fathers (and mothers) carry an enormous amount of transgenerational entanglements that limit their potential to fulfill their God-given roles as fathers. After all, a father can only pass on to his children what he received from his parents and those who came before him. What he from his own father is especially important here. A father's limitations can leave his child seeking protection and provision outside the family and the consequences of this seeking can be devastating and far-reaching.

How your father was able to fulfill his role as the first man in your life, his choices, and his behavior have left a significant imprint on you — body, heart, and soul. If you carry a buried, or not so buried, father wound know there is hope. The transgenerational entanglements that blocked or blunted your father's ability to father you as God originally intended can be turned around. If your father was really good at the father thing—great! You are blessed indeed, and my heart celebrates with you. Perhaps it is this blessing that lies at the core of an inner calling to be of greater service to the world around you.

The "father wound," as I call it, is the pain experienced when one grows up without the earthy father love their hearts yearn for. So who is this first man in your life, the man who you would measure all other men against? Where did he carry what was handed down to him from his father and his father before him? If he experienced pain in his early life, did he succumb to alcoholism, drugs, workaholism, anger, rage, control, indifference, or apathy, or perhaps was he not present in the lives of his children? To accept him as he is lends itself to your own self-acceptance. After all, you are half your father. His blood runs through your veins, and you carry his DNA. To fight against these facts creates struggle within. This struggle can appear impossible to overcome.

ACCEPTANCE: THE KEY TO FREEDOM

Accepting your father does not require your agreement with all of his behavior. However, perhaps recognizing that your father is doing the best he can do given his life experiences will prove helpful. We are all affected by the relationships we share with others, and these relationships mold our subconscious mind and subsequent behavior. Fathers are no exception here. I too had to accept my father for who he was before I could have peace of heart.

THE JESUS CODE CONNECTION
Father – Protector - Provider

HAROLD LEE BULLARD

My father was known as Lee Bullard to most; however, to me, he was the man from whom I wanted fatherly love. However, my dad was tormented by a long list of subconscious files that separated him from living the life God had for him, and he was unable to give me what my heart longed for – daddy love. I strongly suspect that he was a very wounded Enneagram Eight individual. When Enneagram Eight individuals are trapped in their wounds they can be very violent, revengeful, and downright scary individuals. They carry a huge, and sometimes very scary, energy. They become the loud roaring lion in the room.

You see, my dad was a rather angry, belittling man, who was a self-proclaimed atheist who didn't know Jesus during my childhood (fortunately he did come to know Jesus later in his life; however, that is a story for another time). My dad would fly off the handle without warning and his anger forced me to stuff and hide my desire for his love. He was also a brilliant mathematician and engineer with the spirit of an entrepreneur, who continually sought to create businesses. Under it all, you would occasionally see the little boy who wanted to be loved – the teddy bear who wanted to love and care for others. Like all deeply wounded Enneagram Type Eight individuals, his core need to "be against" set him against the people around him. His revenge type anger kept him isolated from the love he desired.

Unfortunately, my dad was emotionally absent from my life, and I always felt the pangs of unrequited fatherly love, protection, and provision. It's no surprise I became a single teenage mother at age eighteen. I was looking for love in every place guaranteed to not give me love. My daughter's father left us when she was only five months old, and the pattern of unrequited father love continued in my family. My search for healing of my "father wound" led me down a path of miraculous transformation which, in the end, served to more deeply unite my heart with the heart of Jesus. I would like to share with you the pivotal piece that facilitated this healing of my heart—the Family Constellation that changed my life with Peter and Jamie Faust.

My Father's Constellation

The session took place during a The Constellation Approach workshop in the Fall of 2014. As I sat with the group, the time to work on my buried father pain arose, and Jami invited me to the front of the room. The session began with a brief sharing of my story with the group. Jami facilitated the session beautifully. Upon hearing my story, Jami determined that I needed to select someone to proxy for my dad, my paternal grandfather, and my paternal great grandfather. While much happened during the constellation, there were two key moments that I want to share with you in this book. One component centered around my father's anger, and the other healed the unrequited father love my heart yearned for.

Once the constellation began, I stood in the center of the room looking at the man who was the proxy for my dad. Immediately I felt frozen, unable to move. I became the fearful little child who could not move toward her father. Since I have done this work before, I knew I needed to move toward my dad's proxy to facilitate healing; however, I simply couldn't take a step toward him. There was a piece of my buried pain that needed to be addressed first. This piece was my father's anger, the part of him I always wished would go away so that he could love me. His anger served as an impenetrable force field between us. At this point, Jami, witnessing my struggle, asked another attendee to proxy for my dad's anger. Soon this proxy was standing next to my dad, staring directly at me. I remember looking at her, straight in the eye, and thinking to myself "There is no way you are coming past me and harming my family or my children. Step back!" I was going to fight anger with force.

> All I needed to do was ask and then allow Jesus to transform this anger into love.

Boy was I trying to fight fire with fire—which never works by the way. Eventually I knew I couldn't do this on my own, so I prayed. I asked Jesus to heal my family of this anger. I knew that only Jesus could handle this battle. Then it happened; I saw the truth. My dad's anger could be transformed—I did not need to fight it. All I needed to do was ask and then allow Jesus to transform this anger into love. Then I prayed, asking Jesus to take this anger and transform it into love. At that moment, everything changed. The room softened, my gaze softened, and the proxy for my dad's anger softened. Eventually I found myself able to begin moving toward the man who was standing in for my dad.

After a series of healing statements directed by Jami, I eventually felt the urge to hug my "dad." At one point during our hug, I looked up at him as tears were rolling down my face. It was at that point I understood a bit of what my dad carried in his life and how much he did indeed love me. I understood his wounds held him back from loving me, and it was OK—God was filling in where my earthly father couldn't do it. Jami's soft words sounded as if an angel was speaking: "That's right, Carolyn, take in all the father love your heart has wanted for all those years." This is precisely what I did. I stayed in his arms, allowing God to fill my heart with all the father love I could ever desire. Eventually I was able to release, step back and tell my "dad," "Thank you for giving me life. What you gave me was enough for me to live a happy, abundant life, and you are the right dad for me." At that point, it was as if a blanket of father love enveloped me and all was right in the world.

> *Psalm 34:18 - The Lord is near to the*
> *brokenhearted, and saves the crushed in spirit.*

This Family Constellation was many years ago, and my heart is still full of father love today. I now think of my dad with fondness, and I am able to see more clearly why he did what he did during his lifetime. Additionally, I now regularly pray for his soul. My heart is filled with happiness and love when I reserve Masses for him, when I pray for him, and when I reflect on how hard he tried to find happiness during his lifetime. I know my dad is being healed by the one true healer, Jesus Christ. I am grateful he is my dad. I accept the painful times because through that pain I am able to love others with a deeper understanding and clarity. May your soul rest in peace Harold Lee Bullard. I know you are looking down on me with fatherly pride. See you again someday, much much later. Your loving daughter—Carolyn Marie (Bullard) Berghuis.

> *Exodus 20:12 - "Honor your father and your*
> *mother, that your days may be long in the land*
> *which the Lord your God gives you."*

GOD IS CLOSE TO THE BROKENHEARTED

Perhaps your earthly father struggles to find the freedom and joy his heart desires; however, the father love that only a sinless father can offer is available to each and every one of us. God will protect and provide abundantly for his children who seek him. And seek him we must because this seeking will indeed lead us to the healing our hearts yearn for. The key is perseverance and surrender. Remember, our Father in heaven is close to the brokenhearted. At those moments when we need him the greatest, he is there. Father God has certainly been there for me.

> God will protect and provide abundantly for his children who seek him.

> *John 4:23-24 - "But the hour is coming, and now is,*
> *when the true worshipers will worship the Father*
> *in spirit and truth, for such the Father seeks to*
> *worship him. God is spirit, and those who worship*
> *him must worship in spirit and truth."*

My own father had his battles while alive. These battles affected our family profoundly. Whatever your struggles are with your father, know that they can be healed. I have seen it in my life, and I have seen it in the lives of many others. The pain you experienced with your father can lead you down a path toward greater love, appreciation, and acceptance of others and the world around you. Who knows what gifts will be illuminated as you heal your father wound. More on your father's role in the family in Chapter 13, "Mother as Nurturer and Comforter."

THE JESUS CODE CONNECTION
Heavenly Father – Heals - Loves

« Chapter 11 »

The 7th Face of Struggle: Anxiety and Depression

Romans 8: 35, 37 - Who shall separate us from the love of Christ? Shall tribulation, or distress, or persecution, or famine, or nakedness, or peril, or sword? No, in all these things we are more than conquerors through him who loved us.

I n the world today, many individuals live in a constant state of anxiety or depression at some level that can grow into full-blown panic attacks, anxiety disorders, or clinical depression when the right set of circumstances are met. The National Institute of Mental Health (NIH) offers the following disturbing statistics in the United Sates in 2014:

Adults

(only 58.7% of adults with a serious mental illness received treatment).

- 18.1% of all adults suffered from an anxiety disorder in the past year.

- 6.7 % of all adults had at least one major depressive episode in the past year.

- 4.2% of all adults suffered a serious mental illness.

- 3.5% of all adults have suffered PTSD (post-traumatic stress disorder).

- 64.2% of jail inmates suffered from a mental health problem. (data from 2004)

Children

(only 50.6% received treatment for mental health issues, only 32.2% with anxiety)

- 25.1% of all 13–18 year olds have suffered from an anxiety disorder in the past year.

- 11.4% of all 12–17 year olds had at least one major depressive episode in the past year.

- 4.0% of 13–18 years olds have suffered PTSD (post-traumatic stress disorder).

- 2.7% of 13–18 year olds have suffered from an eating disorder.

We have a serious problem in the United States and the world today, and in light of the promises of Christ, I find these numbers disturbing and extremely saddening. We see in the book of Hosea, God rebuking the people of Israel because they had lost their way. They were "swearing, lying, committing murder, stealing, committing adultery, and bloodshed followed bloodshed" across the land. Basically, they were abandoning God's law. God was especially poignant with the priests who were not instructing the people properly, leaving them without hope and proper direction to God.

> *Hosea 4:6 - "My people are destroyed for lack of knowledge; because you have rejected knowledge, I reject you from being a priest to me. And since you have forgotten the law of your God, I also will forget your children."*

Remember Job? The man who suffered loss beyond what most of us can imagine? Also, do you remember how faithful Job was to God through his trials? Yes, Job stumbled a bit – most of us would if we were walking in his footsteps. However, Job was faithful to God through all his loss and God, was faithful to Job. God will be faithful to us too.

> *Job 36:11-12 - "If they listen, and serve him, they complete their days in prosperity, and their years in pleasantness. But if they do not listen, they shall perish by the sword, and die without knowledge."*

You see, we are not very different from the Israelites. We still sin and as a result we still suffer. However, unlike the Israelites in Hosea and even Job himself, we have been given a savior who came to seek and save the lost—Jesus Christ. He came to show us how to have life and have it to the fullest. He is the one who came to give us peace of mind and heart.

> *John 16:22-24 - "So you have pain now; but I will see you again, and your hearts will rejoice, and no one will take your joy from you. On that day you will ask nothing of me. Very truly, I tell you, if you ask anything of the Father in my name, he will give it to you. Until now you have not asked for anything in my name. Ask and you will receive, so that your joy may be complete."*

Given the multifaceted dimension of these issues, including the fact that we now have Christ in our hearts—the antidote to all sin and subsequent pain—a holistic approach that addresses the physical, emotional, and spiritual component is required in order to change the pattern, and experience real peace and happiness. In other words, it's time to take another approach to the pain in humanity's broken heart.

In Chapter 5, we looked at the effect emotions have on our well-being. Additionally, in Chapter 6, "The Stages of Healing," we looked at depression and learned just how close we are to happiness when we are in it. In this chapter, we are going to look a little deeper into anxiety and depression specifically so that you can develop a deeper understanding of these issues from a physical, emotional, and spiritual point of view. After all, given the statistics from 2014 (I assume they are getting worse each year), mankind is in need of a massive shift.

THE PHYSICAL COMPONENT

When looking to balance the physical aspect of anxiety and depression, we must properly support a variety of hormones and biochemicals in our body, including vitality hormones, stress hormones, and brain chemicals. This is done by identifying and supporting the needs of your endocrine system, your limbic system, and your digestive system. Your endocrine system consists of glands like your thyroid and adrenals that produce your vitality hormones including estrogen, progesterone, testosterone, DHEA, thyroid hormones, cortisol, and insulin. Keeping them properly balanced is essential for optimal peace of mind. Your limbic system includes those structures of the brain that regulate your emotional responses to stress, including your hypothalamus and amygdala. Lastly, your digestive system has a significant role in creating serotonin, a specific neurotransmitter needed for peace of mind. While going into detail on the physical component of transformation is beyond the scope of this book, it is important to understand that a whole body approach, including supporting your physical body, is essential if you want to live fully alive. In the Appendix, you will find a listing of recommended books in this area.

BODY AND BRAIN CHEMICALS

Your neurotransmitters (brain chemicals) play a huge role in your emotional health. Keeping your neurotransmitters such as serotonin, dopamine, and GABA in balance is important if you are to experience peace and happiness. Here is a quick rundown on key neurotransmitters as they relate to different mental states.

Key Neurotransmitters

- *Dopamine:* is critical to central nervous system functions such as movement, pleasure, attention, mood, and motivation. It strongly resembles noradrenaline.

- *Serotonin:* can affect mood and social behavior, appetite and digestion, sleep, memory, and sexual desire and function. Eighty to ninety percent of it can be found in the gastrointestinal tract.

- *Oxytocin:* is the bonding/attachment hormone that creates feelings of calm and closeness. It is released during breastfeeding and childbirth as well as during intimacy in both sexes.

- *Noradrenaline:* is a stress hormone released during the fight or flight response that increases heart rate and blood pressure, widens air passages in the lungs, and narrows blood vessels in non-essential organs.

- *Adrenaline:* is an adrenal hormone released during acute stress. It is similar to noradrenaline in its effects.

Mental States and Neurotransmitters

- *During periods of happiness:* high serotonin levels are produced.

- *During moments of love:* high and balanced levels of dopamine, serotonin, and oxytocin are produced.

- *During moments of anxiety:* low dopamine is present.

- *During periods of depression:* low dopamine and low serotonin levels are evident.

- *During times of stress (fight or flight):* very high noradrenaline and high adrenaline are produced.

- *When suffering from schizophrenia:* very high dopamine levels are evident.

While an in-depth discussion of the endocrine system and neurotransmitters is again outside the scope of this book, there are practitioners who specialize in this type of care, and fortunately, the field is expanding.

If you or a loved one are suffering from anxiety, depression, or any other neurological health issue, I highly recommend that you seek the care of a qualified health care practitioner skilled in neurotransmitter and endocrine support.

THE ENNEAGRAM AND ANXIETY

In Chapter 5 we looked at the unique relationship Enneagram types Two, Three, and Four have with shame and in Chapter 6 we discussed the unique relationship Enneagram types Eight, Nine, and One have with the emotion of anger. While all of us experience shame and anger from time to time, it particularly pronounced when these individuals are under stress. Similarly, individuals who identify with Enneagram types Five, Six, or Seven carry underlying levels of anxiety when they are stressed, especially when they are still trapped in their wounds. Like the emotion of shame or anger, feelings of anxiety are not limited to Enneagram types Five, Six, and Seven; however, a brief examination into these types will be helpful.

First, recall that the use of the word "stress" here points to an emotional or physical state that takes us away from wholeness, periods of time when we move away from our true-self. It is much more than being "stressed out." For Enneagram types Five, Six, and Seven, those in the Head Triad, anxiety is their go-to emotion when they are under stress. They are our thinking types who struggle with contacting their inner guidance.

Type Five individuals are the world's insightful thinkers, they want to understand why things work the way they do. They deeply desire to find truth for themselves. Think philosopher, theologian, or scientist here. You seldom find them without a book. They seem to always be involved in some form of study or investigation. They move inward with their thoughts and they have a basic desire to be competent and capable. Feeling incapable or useless will cause great stress for them. Albert Einstein, Stephen Hawking, Bill Gates and Mark Zuckerberg are all examples of individuals who identify with Enneagram Type Five. When these individuals are under stress their anxiety will likely cause them to become both detached and intense. At that point they retreat to their safe space – inside their head and away from others.

Individuals who identify with Enneagram Type Six are cautious people who seek support and security. They are also great troubleshooters who can beautifully foster group cooperation. If you need someone to count on you can count on a Type Six, providing they trust you and see you as part of their group. Once you have gained the trust of a Type Six you have a true blue friend indeed. When they fear a lack of support and guidance they become stressed and their anxiety arises. A few notable Enneagram Type Six individuals are Edgar Hoover, Richard Nixon, George H.W. Bush, Robert F. Kennedy, Malcom X, Princess Diana, and Marilyn Monroe. When they are stressed they over think and they worry – a lot! They become afraid to make decisions and they do not want to be controlled by others. When under stress their biggest fear of being alone without support can get the better of them and separate them from peace and happiness.

Type Seven individuals are our optimistic extroverts. They are fun – always attracted to the next shiny thing that crosses their path. They bring life to any party and they intrinsically see the world through the lens of childlike excitement. They are the quintessential FOMO (fear of missing out) people. They are quick witted because their mindset is anticipatory – always looking forward. Examples of notable Type Seven individuals include Amelia Earhart, John F. Kennedy, Joe Biden, Sarah Palin, Britney Spears, and Mick Jagger.

When under stress Type Seven's fear becoming deprived and in pain and they will express a bit of impatient nerviness.

Regardless of your Enneagram type, anxiety affects all of us. It disturbs our inner peace and it interferes with our ability to move into contemplation and deep prayer – the space where we meet God.

CHANGE YOUR PERCEPTION OF DANGER AND ANXIETY

Remember, your perception is your reality. If you perceive danger or if your mind is thinking about something that causes you anxiety, your body is physically responding as if you are actually experiencing the situation in real time. Given this, thinking about the stressful confrontation you had with your spouse produces the same biochemical picture in your body that you experienced during the actual conversation. How many times do you let your mind fret with thoughts of anxiety? Admittedly, I have let my mind drive me crazy from time to time in the past – even though I am not in the Head Triad. Sometimes it seemed as if I relished in replaying the harmful mental tapes over and over in my mind. Maybe you can relate.

Additionally, your body does not differentiate between witnessing troublesome events in real time or stimuli that are received as a result of artificial exposure. Violent and suspenseful video games, books, and movies can initiate a stress response in the body. Given the developing brain of a child this can be

> If you perceive danger or if your mind is thinking about something that causes you anxiety, your body is physically responding as if you are actually experiencing the situation in real time.

especially troublesome. Repeated harmful patterns can take root in the subconscious mind of a child rather easily. With repetition these patterns can begin to feel "normal" when indeed they should not be perceived as normal. This type of exposure incites the danger/excitatory hormones and neurotransmitters that are designed to alarm you in the case of danger. Overexposure to these biochemicals contributes to a long list of physical and emotional health issues. Stress is significant, and we have more control over our stress response than we realize. We must begin by limiting our exposure.

> *Romans 8:6 - To set the mind on the flesh is death,*
> *but to set the mind on the Spirit is life and peace.*

Your brain is not at its best when you are experiencing anxiety. You are created to relish in the things of God and what God created. A reflection on the internal peace you feel while gazing at the stars or a sunset, or taking a stroll through a garden will remind you of this fact.

> *Psalm 96:11-12 - Let the heavens be glad, and let*
> *the earth rejoice; let the sea roar, and all that fills*
> *it; let the field exult, and everything in it. Then shall*
> *all the trees of the forest sing for joy.*

THE JESUS CODE CONNECTION
Your Physical Body Needs Spiritual Support

CREATING A BIT OF HEAVEN ON EARTH

Now think for a moment about beautiful music or art. How does it make you feel when you sit in awe of a masterpiece created by a gifted and skilled artist, someone who has discovered their innate God-given gifts and has taken the time and care to cultivate them? How does it make you feel when you listen to beautiful music? Does it take you away from life's stressors, demands, and frustrations? I personally feel uplifted when I listen to Christian music and I play it throughout my home almost every day—almost continuously. When I do this I am allowing words and music that praise Jesus to enter my conscious and subconscious mind. If you are a mother or father of young, impressionable children, you may want to do this in your home as well. This is a great gift you can give your children, a powerful counter to the subconscious programming they will receive from the world.

God has blessed each and every one of us with unique gifts—gifts he gave us so that we can fulfill our role in the creation of his universe. You have been given beautiful gifts too, gifts that bring forth a portion of God's beauty into the world. But their expression will be hindered at some level if you carry burdens in your own heart.

> *1 Corinthians 12:4-7 - Now there are varieties of gifts, but the same Spirit; and there are varieties of services, but the same Lord; and there are varieties of activities, but it is the same God who activates all of them in everyone. To each is given the manifestation of the Spirit for the common good.*

THE JESUS CODE CONNECTION
Your Gifts Matter

HAPPINESS, PEACE AND PHYSIOLOGY

Like anxiety, a person does not necessarily need to be in the middle of a significant loss to experience the physiology of depression. Have you ever watched a sad movie or learned of a heart-wrenching real-life story and experienced the welling up of tears? If so, your body responded as if you were actually experiencing the event in current time. My advice is this: protect your heart from these types of experiences as much as possible by making a conscious decision to introduce happiness, humor, and levity into your life. The world will give you enough struggles. You don't

> Laughter is indeed good medicine.

need to give them to yourself. Laughter is indeed good medicine. I invite you to consider what activities you can introduce into your life that will support greater happiness and peace. Then start to introduce them. Read uplifting materials. Listen to uplifting Christian music. Visit an art museum. Visit your church. Spend time with your spouse, children, or grandchildren. The list of possibilities is endless and beautiful.

> Individuals with the healthiest spiritual lives enjoy the greatest levels of well-being when they engage in a wellness program.

Proverbs 4:23 - Keep your heart with all vigilance, for from it flow the springs of life.

KEEPING IT REAL: PHYSICAL, EMOTIONAL, AND SPIRITUAL HEALTH

As I mentioned before, in addition to introducing activities that foster happiness and peace in your life, it is also important to support your physical body. After all, you do live in a physical body that needs to be cared for. Illness and lack of vitality in your physical body can serve to hinder your movement toward happiness and peace. It's hard to feel good emotionally when your body hurts physically. However, what about the saints that suffer physical ailments while experiencing profound unity with Jesus Christ? After all, there is a very long list of these individuals—individuals who have reached a level of perfection the rest of us have not reached. They have reached the Seventh Stage of Healing—Love Consuming—as discussed in Chapter 6.

My many years of experience as a naturopath have taught me that there are three essential steps that must be fulfilled before you can experience optimal levels of well-being. First, you must supply your body with the correct nutrients needed for the formation of necessary biochemicals and avoid as much as possible the toxins that harm you. This will help create and maintain healthy tissues, organs, and glands that create your hormones, neurotransmitters, and other body chemicals. Second, you must engage in activities that support emotional health such as reading and listing to uplifting material, and cultivate healthy relationships in your life. However, the biggest piece to well-being will not be found in the physical world. It is found in the space where God resides, the place of highest importance. You must engage in activities that support your spiritual health. Activities such as prayer, meditation, and time spent alone with God, will support you on this transformational journey.

> You must engage in activities that support your spiritual health such as prayer, meditation, and time with God, in order for your body to function optimally.

THE THREE COMPONENTS OF OPTIMAL WELLNESS

1. Your physical health

2. Your emotional health

3. Your spiritual health

Over the years, I have worked with thousands of individuals who have sought more out of life, more health, happiness and peace. Through it all I have observed that individuals who place significant importance on living spiritually healthy lives enjoy the greatest levels of well-being. In other words, these individuals give primacy to their spiritual health over their physical health. When we focus on our physical health first, we are putting the cart ahead of the horse so to speak. Our spiritual life comes first, our emotional life flows from our spiritual life, and our physical life is supported by both. We must first seek God through Jesus in the perfect love of the Holy Spirit.

THE HOLY TRINITY

We live in a sea of infinite love and pure potentiality. Let's paint a picture. Imagine a little fish in the ocean, floating around and bathing in the waters. The little fish breathes in this life giving water effortlessly. Water fills every part of this little fish and yet, the little fish is unaware of the water. Not only is the fish unaware of the life giving water, it has no clue that it would die outside of it. Without the water there is no life for the little fish.

Now let's pause for a bit and think about the Holy Trinity. Father God is the one who created the water, the little fish, and the entire ocean. He perfectly orchestrated everything so that the little fish could live. Once Father God created the little fish it came into being through the Son. Then gazing at their creation together, the Father and the Son share an infinite divine love that envelops their little fish. Much like two parents gazing at their sleeping child, a special love lives between them. This divine love is the Holy Spirit.

The same is true for us. Except we are created in the image of our Triune God. God the Father created every human being in his love. Then he willed all of us into life through his Son. Together, God the Father and God the Son adore and love each of us. They continually gaze upon us with a divine love that immerses us - the Holy Spirit.

> 1 John 5:11 - God gave us eternal life, and this life is
> in his Son. Whoever has the Son has life; whoever
> does not have the Son of God does not have life.

The Holy Trinity loved everything into existence from a sacred space – the root of all creation. From this root our Triune God can create everything and anything. It is the divine field of pure potentiality.

We are like the little fish swimming in the Holy Spirit's loving water. This love immerses our cells and keeps us alive. We breath in this water every moment of our life and it fills every part of us – every cell. This water holds each and every person on our planet and it gives life to all. Without this sacred water we cannot live, that is, without God's perfect love we will die. Every time we sin or participate in an unloving act a part of us dies for lack of this life giving water. And every time we allow love to enter in we receive life. God's life giving water surrounds us and we can always allow it in to heal any broken pieces of ourselves.

We need to return to the well of living water time and time again. Like the woman at the well, we will live when we drink of it. We return to the well every time we love. Prayer, especially Contemplative Prayer, is an essential piece towards restoration of love. If you would like to learn more about Contemplative Prayer I invite you to visit my website: www.TheLIVEMethod.com.

> *John 4:14-15 – "But whoever drinks of the water that I shall give him will never thirst; the water that I shall give him will become in him a spring of water welling up to eternal life." The woman said to him, "Sir, give me this water, that I may not thirst, nor come here to draw."*

TRUE LIFE

This is why our saints can live lives fully alive within a physical body that is ill, weak, or diseased. They know they have been given life by the Father, through the Son and that they live in the milieu of the Holy Spirit. They drink the true healing water of Jesus Christ. Looking at the life of Saint Mother Teresa of Calcutta, we witness this wisdom. Saint Teresa of Calcutta suffered physically, yet this little lady was a strong force for the Lord. She was a highly evolved Enneagram Type Eight who took care of her people. She worked hard to meet their physical needs; however, she also worked tirelessly to meet their greatest need – their need to know and love God. Great saints like Saint Teresa sought God first in all matters, and through their physical and emotional trials, they found him in a deep and profound way, a way that led to their perfection. Through their state of perfection they ushered healing into the world.

For the rest of us, we are not yet strong enough to withstand significant physical or emotional assaults on our body and remain spiritually strong through our trials. Trials tend to separate most of humanity from God rather than forging a more beautiful union, and that is OK. We are all a work in progress.

It is important to appreciate and honor where we are right now, what we have accomplished, and what we have been through up until this point in our lives. Where you are right now is where you are called to be, yet God has more for you. Our infinite God always has more. Your trials present an opportunity to become more beautifully united with him. We are all called to be saints. All saints began like you and me—a human being living in the world, experiencing torments and trials while trying to find a better way.

> **Breath of Christ**
>
> Breath in: I
>
> Breath out: love
>
> Breath in: you
>
> Breath out: Jesus

THE JESUS CODE CONNECTION
Physical – Emotional – Spiritual

BREATH OF CHRIST MEDITATION

This is one of my favorite meditations, and I have found it very helpful when I need to shift out of a negative emotion into greater happiness. This meditation came to me one day while in the perpetual adoration chapel at my church. I was sitting there in the stillness, following my breath as a means to quiet and settle my mind, when Jesus came and spoke to me again.

As I was sitting there with Jesus, it occurred to me that there is great power in speaking the words "I love you" to Jesus. As I sat there, my heart became aware of the goodness that speaking these words offer. Speaking "I love you" to Jesus opens a door where he can bless you with greater goodness, especially when done quietly and slowly, allowing your body a bit of respite.

Imagine for a moment how it feels when someone you love speaks the words "I love you" with heartfelt love. Perhaps, if you are a parent, imagine your child telling you that he or she loves you—like the little girl who picked flowers for her mom in Chapter 2. How does your heart respond? Do you want to fill your little child's heart with happiness and peace? Of course you do. In light of this, can you begin to imagine what happens when you stand before Jesus, the one who you came into being through? What could his Sacred Heart, pulling from the infinite vastness of his universe, possibly want to give you when you slow down and take the time to tell him you love him?

This meditation is easy and simple, and it has a beautiful calming effect on your body, heart, and spirit. To begin the meditation, I suggest sitting calmly with your feet planted on the ground, or lying down. Take your first breath in, slowly, and say, "I." Then gently breathe out and say, "love." Breathe in again, "you," then out, "Jesus." Repeat as many times as you desire. It's beautifully simple, and it deeply unites you with Jesus. You are taking time to speak his "love language" to him. He wants to spend time with you. Remember, Jesus' ways are not burdensome, and they are not difficult. Rather his ways are gentle, sweet, and light.

> *Matthew 11:28-30 - "Come to me, all you who are weary and burdened, and I will give you rest. Take my yoke upon you and learn from me, for I am gentle and humble in heart, and you will find rest for your souls. For my yoke is easy and my burden is light."*

I - Love - You – Jesus

I invite you to share Breath of Christ with your loved ones, practice it with your children as they leave the house for school in the morning and before bed, and share it with your friends—whoever you believe needs a little peace in their life. A client of mine has incorporated Breath of Christ into the wellness program she spearheads at her church. She often ends the group workout classes with Breath of Christ, to center the minds and hearts of her students, setting them to go out into the world centered on the love of Jesus.

BREATH OF CHRIST FOR RESPITE MEDITATION

This meditation uses Breath of Christ to help bring resolution to painful moments of your life. With each numbered step that follows, allow yourself to repeat the necessary number of Breath of Christ cycles that you need to feel comfortable, before you move on to the next step.

- **First Step:** Find a quiet space where you can practice this visualization, and make yourself comfortable.

- **Second Step:** Start breathing several cycles of Breath of Christ to calm your body.

- **Third Step:** Recall your painful moment and notice where in your body you are holding it, remembering Jesus wants to take away your pain.

- **Forth Step:** Gently invite your pain into your hands and see it there.

- **Fifth Step:** Visualize Jesus standing in front of you.

- **Sixth Step:** Look into the eyes of Jesus and allow yourself to see his love for you.

- **Seventh Step:** Look more closely at Jesus. Notice his face more clearly. Look at his arms and outstretched hands.

- **Eighth Step:** Place the pain that you have been holding in your hands into Jesus's hands and look at his face as he receives it.

- **Ninth Step:** Continue Breath of Christ as you do this. Continue to tell Jesus you love him.

- **Tenth Step:** Now bow your head to Jesus in gratitude and allow yourself to feel the infinite love he has for you, the love he wants to give to you as he receives your pain.

- **Eleventh Step:** Allow him to take the pain away and place it on his cross.

- **Twelfth Step:** Once Jesus has placed your pain on his cross, ask him to fill you up with his healing love flowing directly from his Sacred Heart so that you become free to live the life he desires for you, a life of peace and happiness.

- **Thirteenth Step:** Receive this gift of love from Jesus, and experience it entering into the place where the pain once lived—the pain you gave to Jesus.

- **Last Step:** Allow his peace to overcome you, and enjoy this sacred time with Jesus.

Remember, the pain will lift in perfect order, as Jesus desires for your spiritual growth toward him—in his perfect timing. The journey through the pain will then become a sacred journey you experience with him that will lead you to the Father.

> *Psalm 147:3 - He heals the brokenhearted and binds up their wounds.*

THE JESUS CODE CONNECTION
I – Love – You - Jesus

FROM MY HEART TO YOURS

You are created in the image of God, your maker who desires your happiness and wholeness. However, you live in a world riddled with challenges that you must move through if you are going to experience the life your heart desires—the life God has for you. These challenges include physical challenges, emotional challenges, and most importantly, they include spiritual challenges. Life's challenges can facilitate great growth, providing we move through them with God's grace. Never have I had a client come to me and tell me they experienced their greatest gratitude in the easy times in their lives. Rather, many, many clients over the years have shared with me the profound gratitude they have for their strife and struggles. These were the periods where they experienced the greatest emotional and spiritual growth. Their struggles eventually led them into greater peace, joy, and happiness. Then they were free to experience heightened gratitude for the little (and easy) things in life.

Offering gratitude for the blessings in your life is one of the most beautiful ways you can foster greater happiness. Because, remember, gratitude and love are not congruent with painful emotions like shame, anger, or anxiety. Perhaps creating a journal of the things you love and are grateful for will help you on your journey toward happiness and peace. Or feel free to write these down in the blank pages at the end of this book.

> *Proverbs 12:25 - Anxiety in a man's heart weighs him down, but a good word makes him glad.*

We know that Jesus promised us that his yoke is easy and his burden is light. While this runs contrary to the anxiety and depression we witness in the world today, his words are true. Go to him, turn to him, create a space for him in your life so that he can reach you. I invite you to create an altar in your home with a candle, your Bible, or other Christian materials, where you commit to spending a set amount of time with God, praying and meditating when you feel called. It doesn't even need to be a large amount of time. It's consistency that counts. Consistency will change your life. Like any relationship with a loved one, you need to commit to the relationship and spend time with your beloved for your love to deepen and grow.

> Practice speaking words of truth over your life and the lives of your loved ones—words that are true in the eyes of God.

Lastly, be ever mindful of the words you speak. They have great power in your life and the lives of your loved ones. They can cut, or they can heal. They can be used for your good—or for your harm. Practice speaking words of truth over your life and the lives of your loved ones— words that are true in the eyes of God. Words of love, forgiveness, and acceptance that express the truth of God's vision for your life. In Chapter 14, "The Language of LIVE Within The Nine Faces of Struggle," I will share with you helpful phrases that will nourish your heart and soul to help you draw you closer to Christ.

> *Ephesians 4:29 - Let no evil talk come out of your mouths, but only what is useful for building up, as there is need, so that your words may give grace to those who hear.*

THE JESUS CODE CONNECTION
Challenges – Gratitude - Words

« Chapter 12 »

The 8th Face of Struggle: Addictions, Religion, and God

1 Peter 5:10 -And after you have suffered for a little while, the God of all grace, who has called you to his eternal glory in Christ, will himself restore, support, strengthen, and establish you.

M ake no mistake about it, addictions steal lives. They rip families apart, preying upon the deepest yearning we have for belonging and our deep need to love and be loved in return. They steal fathers, mothers, sons, daughters, brothers, and sisters from their loved ones. They rip families apart and leave in their wake a battlefield of isolation, shame, and guilt. Lives that were meant to be filled with joy, hope, and love become hijacked when the initial allure of addiction presents itself.

ADDICTIONS' FALSE PROMISES

At first, the addiction is subtle, briefly flashing before your heart, revealing what your heart deeply yearns for in an attempt to garner a second look. A promise to belong, a promise of escape, or a promise of love is offered to you. It's as if the addiction knows what your heart so desperately needs, and it knows how to entice and seduce your heart. However, the addiction must work hard and fast in order to confuse your heart and convince it to accept its false promises.

Like the thief who comes in the night seeking only to steal, kill, and destroy, addiction must enter under cover so as to gain entry into your heart. It must cover the sinister falsities and lies that are found at its core because to reveal them would cause you to flee. You see, at addiction's core, you will find a fearful energy propelled into motion out of a deep hatred of love itself. This dark energy drives addiction to maneuver as it attempts to commit thievery under the cover of false promises. Addiction offers false promises of love, of life, and of light, when all the while it secretly desires to destroy these very things. Addiction, being propelled by the angel of light, the fallen archangel Satan himself, understands the power of love, and uses your innate desire for love against you. You see, addiction seeks nothing more than to steal your birthright and rightful inheritance God has given you as his child.

> Addiction seeks nothing more than to steal your birthright and rightful inheritance God has given you as his child.

However, you have a shepherd protecting your birthright, and his voice will be heard. Your shepherd, Jesus Christ, knows you, and he seeks you. He will not rest until he brings all of his sheep back home. Once home, you will participate in the love relationship that exists between the Father and the Son. A relationship where only truth and love live.

> John 10:14-16 - "I am the good shepherd. I know my own and my own know me, just as the Father knows me and I know the Father. And I lay down my life for the sheep. I have other sheep that do not belong to this fold. I must bring them also, and they will listen to my voice. So there will be one flock, one shepherd."

> ### THE JESUS CODE CONNECTION
> *Addiction – Thief – Heart*

THE VALUE OF YOUR BEAUTIFUL HEART

Your heart holds infinite value because it is the home the Holy Trinity desires to dwell in. In order to obtain entry into your heart, its currency must be offered—love itself. However, addiction does not authentically hold this currency, so it must lie and steal in an attempt to gain ownership. Given its disordered nature, addiction steals love from you, and in return, it falsely offers it back as a gift. Addiction knows your dreams of a better life, a happier life, a life of peace and love, and it offers the promise of their fulfillment. It knows that you desire love. Once your relationship with addiction is consummated, you will unknowingly surrender love at addiction's feet.

Now your heart, held in bondage, begins to harden to protect itself from the pain addiction inflicts. Your heart begins to allow in false and limiting beliefs as harmful emotions take up residence within it. You begin to believe you are unable to experience love to its fullest, or perhaps you now settle for less—falsely believing life has nothing more to offer. These are all lies fed by the addiction and fueled by the Evil One. Your heart is created to love and be loved in return. Your heart can love to the fullest. Love has greater power, and it cannot be suppressed by the false lies addiction offers.

> *Ezekiel 36:26 -"A new heart I will give you, and a new spirit I will put within you; and I will remove from your body the heart of stone and give you a heart of flesh."*

Love is powerful and beautiful, and it is what your inner self craves, yet addiction hijacks love and leaves you in a constant state of searching. Like a gerbil on a gerbil wheel, you can't see the end you seek. It is true, nothing compares to pure love, yet addiction appears to have supervened love in the hearts of hundreds of millions of individuals across the world. How can this be? How can we believe that anything other than love can fill the space in our hearts—hearts that only love can perfectly fill? The answer lies in the depth of humanity's wounds.

CHILDHOOD PAIN AND ABUSE

> *Luke 15:6-7 - "And when he comes home, he calls together his friends and his neighbors, saying to them, 'Rejoice with me, for I have found my sheep which was lost.' Just so, I tell you, there will be more joy in heaven over one sinner who repents than over ninety-nine righteous persons who need no repentance."*

Our need for love runs deep, and the pain that interrupts love can first be found in our family and in our churches, the two places where we experience the deep needs of protection, provision, comfort, and nurture. When childhood needs are left unmet, or worse, when we experience the pain of abuse or neglect in our family or church, we are left vulnerable to the false promises of addiction.

For individuals who experienced childhood abuse or neglect, addiction can serve as an escape when the need to deny or minimize the pain that results. To look toward our parents, the individuals we deeply seek love from, and accept their role as perpetrator is too much for our soul to accept. In these cases, escape or denial often seem the only options. Looking toward our childhood church and seeing God interwoven with abuse, fear, or neglect all too often calls us to turn away from God—the only one who can truly heal our pain. This unmet need of parental and Godly love cuts deep and can remain in our heart and soul well into and through adulthood. This type of pain often leaves us unable to fully heal and care for ourselves like an adult. All too often we are left feeling trapped. We remain a child yearning for love and belonging even though we live in the body of an adult. Over the years, the repressed pain will cause our hearts to harden and we will build walls around our precious hearts. This is done in an attempt to protect our heart from further pain, which is understandable. Even then, God's love is ever present and always around us ready to enter in and heal us.

> Psalm 73:26 -My flesh and my heart may fail, but God is the strength of my heart and my portion forever.

Sexual abuse is particularly and profoundly damaging to your soul because it strikes at the very place God intended the most sacred of all human expression of love—sexual intimacy and romantic love. This union of love lies at the center of man-kinds communal nature, and it sits at the foundation of the family. However, instead of God's love entering into this sacred space; shame, betrayal, anger, fear, defenselessness, disgust, and self-hatred patterns gain entry into the heart and mind. Victims of sexual abuse are often left not knowing where to turn to for this most sacred of all love.

Profound pain resulting from sexual abuse can leave you vulnerable to the lies of addiction. Addiction serves as the perfect self-sabotage necessary to prove to the world that you are unworthy of love and you are inherently bad—a false belief that many victims take on. Unfortunately, the world today is all too willing to participate in this falsity. None of these beliefs are true in the eyes of God. You are created in his image, and you are precious to him regardless of what the world tells you.

> Song of Solomon 4:7 - You are altogether beautiful, my love; there is no flaw in you.

THE JESUS CODE CONNECTION
Wholly Loved – Child of God

THE PIERCING PAIN OF BULLYING

Childhood abuse takes many forms and has many perpetrators, from family members to classmates and other adults. As a society, we are beginning to take bullying more seriously than ever before. Bullying can lead to grave consequences for all involved, because at its core exclusion is found. I understand how deep these wounds run, I was a target of bullying in high school. My Catholic high school, where I should have been able to find God, was anything but a safe refuge from the world. Instead of finding God when I needed him most (after the pain of my parent's divorce), I was drawn to seek love in the world. Trying to navigate the heartache of living in a broken, loveless family I was left feeling alone and vulnerable. Remember, I am an Enneagram Type Two and Type Twos hold a core need to be loved and needed. My core fear of not being loved hit hard. I became numb to my need for love. Years of suffering for myself and my oldest daughter were the consequence. While I wasn't lead towards the path of addiction, I was lead down the road of heavy shame, shame that deeply scarred my heart.

For many, addition becomes a safe harbor from bullying. It promises friendship and belonging. It also promises to become a needed wall of protection that hides the pain of being bullied. However, what addiction leaves behind is anything but a safe harbor. It only offers more pain. Only forgiveness will provide a true harbor from the pain inflicted by a perpetrator. The risky behavior that follows addiction actually leaves its victim more vulnerable to further attack – the world can be merciless. Forgiveness on the other hand, offers real freedom and friendship. In the case of Sarah, her addiction left her body ravaged and her self-esteem shattered.

"Sarah"

Sarah came to me in her early thirties. She was a beautiful young wife, and mother of two little boys. After the birth of her second son, according to Sarah, she never "bounced back." She experienced extreme fatigue during the day, and her hair was thinning at an abnormal rate. She had also found it extremely difficult to maintain her current weight. She was eating a very low-calorie diet, a diet that in years past would have produced weight loss. We started addressing the physical needs of her endocrine system; however, I sensed there was much more to her case.

The first thing I noticed about Sarah was her pattern of demeaning herself. She spoke as if she was inherently flawed and not good enough. Statements like "I'll never maintain a healthy weight," "I've never liked my appearance," "If I could lose this baby weight then I would feel better" were common sentiments she shared with me. However, I saw Sarah as an attractive woman who was maintaining a relatively healthy weight.

I suspected an underlying emotional/spiritual component to her health issues, so we scheduled a series of three The LIVE Method appointments. During her first session, she shared with me that her parents divorced when she was nine. She had been an only child, and she alone even before the divorce, but after the divorce, it was worse. Her mom, who she lived with most of the time, worked full time and went back to college after the divorce. Soon after the divorce her dad remarried and had two sons with his new wife. Sarah never felt like she fit in with his new family. She carried a lot of resentment toward her dad because, understandably, she felt he abandonment her and her mom.

In high school, Sarah got a lot of attention from boys. I can only imagine that she was a very pretty young woman—a pretty young woman looking for daddy love. She caught the eye of a fellow. I'll call him John. John was a popular athlete who would eventually make Sarah's high school days a living minefield. His slanderous words cut deep, and they spread far and wide across their high school. He called her fat, ugly, stupid, and he told embellished stories of their sexual relationship to anyone who would listen. As she shared her story with me, tears rolled down her cheeks—some fifteen years later. Sarah had no one to turn to during that time in her life, and she felt all alone as a teenager.

In an attempt to numb the pain, she sought respite in food, and she eventually became bulimic. When the pain would arise, she sought to control it by overindulging in food. This provided temporary comfort and it also offered some sense of control over her life.

However, it didn't take long before Sarah felt the urge to empty her body of the food, and off to the bathroom she went. She was fearful of gaining weight and suffering further bullying as a result. Additionally, she feared becoming unattractive and therefore, in her mind, unlovable. The act of throwing up her food left her feeling shameful, weak, alone, and in her words, "like a weak loser who doesn't deserve to be treated well." Although, she admitted that she felt this was one area in her life where she had control. All of this set the stage for yet another cycle of bulimia. Her shame intensified with every round.

During her sessions, Sarah had many breakthroughs as we worked with the figurines and healing statements. Sarah was persistent. She followed my advice for the most part. Most importantly, she developed a relationship with Jesus and found a nearby church where she became involved. Eventually, Sarah was able to make peace with her dad and his new family. She sought and cultivated a loving relationship with her mother, and the two of them are very close to this day. And regarding the high school boy, she was able to forgive him and accept him for who he was—a fellow human being who was seeking to be loved as well.

Sarah carried many limiting beliefs that separated her from fully living. Much of her pain stemmed from her childhood wounds and the divorce of her parents. The bullying she experienced in high school served to further deepen and solidify her pain. In turn her bulimia created significant shame. If you have experienced life circumstances similar to Sarah then I invite you to determine if the following LIVE statements that Sarah repeated during her LIVE sessions would be of benefit to you.

Key Forgiveness Statements for Sarah

- I forgive myself for believing that I can't be happy without my father's love.

- I forgive myself for believing that I can't love my dad without betraying my mom.

- I forgive myself for believing that I'm ugly and it's ok for people to bully me.

- I forgive myself for believing that if I forgive John, and others who bully, then it gives him and the others permission to bully me again.

- I forgive myself for believing I cannot forgive John.

Mom and Dad Statements

- I leave with my mom and dad what is theirs to carry surrounding their relationship and divorce, and I will carry what is mine to carry.

Spiritual Freedom Statements

- I acknowledge the sense of control I feel when I purge and I call it up from every part of my physical, emotional, and spiritual body and I lay it at the foot of the cross for Jesus to carry it. Now I ask that God, through Jesus, and in the Holy Spirit come into that space and fill it up with divine love so I am free to surrender all control to God and experience all the divine peace God has for me in that space.

- I acknowledge the anger I feel towards my dad when he loves his new family and I call it up from every part of my physical, emotional, and spiritual body and I surrender it at the foot of the cross. Now I ask that God, through Jesus and in the Holly Spirit come into that space and fill it with all the divine Father-daughter love my heart desires so I can feel this love when I love my dad, especially when my dad is loving his new family.

- I acknowledge all of the pain, shame, exclusion, and anger that I felt when I was bullied by John. I call it up and I surrender it at the foot of the cross for Jesus to do with it what he wishes. I unite my pain of being bullied with the pain of being bullied that Jesus felt during his Passion. I proclaim that this pain of mine only serves to help me to love and understand others more fully like Jesus does.

THE CHURCH

> *John 17:20-21 - "I do not ask for these only, but also for those who will believe in me through their word, that they may all be one, just as you, Father, are in me, and I in you, that they also may be in us, so that the world may believe that you have sent me."*

Jesus spoke often about the "world" while he walked the earth as a human being, something mentioned numerous times in this book. In scripture, the "world" is not painted in a positive light, rather the world is portrayed as a place of pain and heartache. Not a big surprise, given who the ruler of this world is—Satan himself. Given the fact that Satan is the ruler of this world it only follows that pain will persist here. This will continue until mankind surrenders completely to God. After all, Satan rejected God and his love. Without God and his love there is no opportunity for true happiness. The pain that you, your loved ones, and the entire human population experiences is the result of Satan's work and mankind's willing collaboration with his evil plan. However, this pain still begets the question, why? Why does God allow Satan to run free like a proud peacock ruling over the creation God so lovingly made?

To understand this, we have to look at sin and our own personal inclinations toward sin. You see, Satan and his fallen angels know our weaknesses, our personal sinful tendencies, and the tendencies of our families. They seek to entice us into sin through these weaknesses. Remember, they were once angels, and when they fell they maintained their angel intellect and keen skills of observation. Fortunately, they cannot read our minds, they can only hear our words. Another reason to be mindful with our words lest they learn too much about our inner thoughts. They know us, and they know which buttons to push to lead us into sin, yet we must exercise our free will to follow them. So why do they want us to sin? Why do they try so hard to entice us into sin?

There is one answer. They have no power to create anything, including a world of their own. They are like parasites living off what God has already created. In an attempt to have a home and world of their own, they must make it a sinful place because they can only exist within sin. Satan and his fallen angels cannot live where love flourishes—this violates God's law. There is no sin whatsoever in heaven, and they no longer belong to heaven. When there is no more sin on earth, they can no longer exist here either.

When Jesus talks about this world, he is talking about the world as it exists because of our sin. I can almost hear the sadness in his voice. He is not saying that Satan is the ultimate ruler or prince by right. Satan is the prince by default, as a result of mankind's sin. And since mankind has given him his throne through sin, we have the power to dethrone him by following the One who is The Way, The Truth, and The Life - Jesus Christ.

> *John 8:31-32 - "If you continue in my word, you are truly my disciples; and you will know the truth, and the truth will make you free."*

THE JESUS CODE CONNECTION
Jesus' Church – God's Children

THE ATTACK

A brief review of church history gives witness to a deep spiritual attack on all forms of Christianity, and in my opinion, a profound spiritual attack on Catholicism in particular. Initially, the early Christians were brutally martyred and tortured for their faith in Jesus Christ. However, the church persisted. Heck, it even flourished. The brutal attacks did not kill this new blossoming religion. However, it didn't take long before dissension and sin entered into the church. One split after another, hate, violence, and anger entered into Mother Church. Yet God desires that we worship together in love.

Hebrews 10:24-25 - And let us consider how to provoke one another to love and good deeds, not neglecting to meet together, as is the habit of some, but encouraging one another, and all the more as you see the Day approaching.

Do you think someone didn't want the church to grow? Do you think Satan and his fallen angels were doing everything possible to snuff out the truth of Jesus Christ? Yes, indeed, they tried, and they have been trying ever since to kill and destroy the church. This is why there now exists over 33,000 different forms of Christianity. All military leaders know the power innate to division. Divide your opponents in an attempt to weaken them, and then strike! We are in the middle of a battlefield my friends. It is time for Christians to come back together and join forces in the spiritual battle. Our participation is essential.

> It is time for Christians to come back together and join forces in the spiritual battle we are in the middle of.

Romans 8:38-39 - For I am sure that neither death, nor life, nor angels, nor principalities, nor things present, nor things to come, nor powers, nor height, nor depth, nor anything else in all creation, will be able to separate us from the love of God in Christ Jesus our Lord.

However, you must remember that Satan's army has only one weapon: our sin. Something our church leaders are not exempt from. Church leaders, like all human beings, have sinned, and the flock has experienced pain as a result. Too many times evil has darkened portions of the hearts of our religious leaders. This is why we must pray for them. We must pray for our churches and those who tend to them. Our church leaders place themselves in harm's way in an attempt to save others, you and I, from physical, emotional, and spiritual pain. They are on the front lines defending us and they need our support and reinforcement. It's no wonder Pope Francis's first request upon accepting the Holy See was our prayers—which he continually requests of us. He knows the power of the Evil One and the intention he has for the world. Pope Francis knows that we are fighting the unseen world and that our greatest weapon is prayer.

Mother Mary has appeared numerous times to mankind, and her message is always consistent: pray and return to her son Jesus Christ. The Rosary is one of the most powerful prayers we can pray. If you are not familiar with it, I invite you to learn of its beauty and power. Saint Padre Pio, a stigmatic and one of our great modern-day saints, called the Rosary his weapon. He prayed it numerous times every day. Some accounts say he prayed it over sixty times a day! In the Appendix are several books I recommend that will help you on your journey in defending the church.

THE JESUS CODE CONNECTION
Defend Mother Church – Pray

WHAT JESUS SET IN MOTION

Jesus, contrary to what some believe and profess, *did* intend to start a new religion. He appointed leaders, he trained them well, and he is still present guiding and defending his church today. To this day, he continues to fortify his followers with his weapons of love, forgiveness, hope, joy, and humility. His delivery source is the Holy Spirit, the advocate who came after him. Jesus gave Saint Peter the keys to the kingdom, and Jesus promised that the netherworld will not overcome. You and I are called to be laborers for Christ, and we are needed.

> *Matthew 16:17-19 - "And I tell you, you are Peter, and on this rock I will build my church, and the gates of Hades will not prevail against it. I will give*

*you the keys of the kingdom of heaven, and
whatever you bind on earth will be bound in
heaven, and whatever you loose on earth will be
loosed in heaven."*

You are a very important part of Christ's body, and you have a unique role to fulfill. Like a beautiful tapestry, you contribute to the beauty of God's creation. Yet to fully step into the life God has for you, you must triumph through your pain, the pain you witness in your family and the pain you see in the world. Up until this point, we have talked about buried wounds and transcending them so you can fully live. We have discussed the importance of prayer, meditation, and turning to Christ. So what is your next step? How are you going to reach your goal of living a life fully alive?

YOUR SPIRITUAL PLAN OF ACTION

Well, you need a plan of action, a blueprint, of sorts, to follow. And like every plan of action, you need to gather a few tools before you get started. You need a drawing board to create your plan on, you need resources to draw upon, you need expert guidance you can trust, and you need a headquarters to work in. And like any excellent leader, you will need to know your strengths and weaknesses. And most importantly, you need to have an intrinsic desire to succeed. And, yes, you are the excellent leader in this life of yours. God has given you free will to steer your ship.

> You are the excellent leader in this life of yours. God has given you free will to steer your ship.

Fortunately, God has also given you the tools necessary to achieve greatness. Make no mistake about it, he has set you up for success. Yet you must choose to follow his lead. He has provided everything you need, and home base is his church. He has placed the resources you need there, he has placed his experts to help and guide within her walls; and most importantly, he has placed at the head of his church the single reason to succeed—his Son Jesus Christ, the light of the world who lives within you!

> *1 Corinthians 12:28-31 - God has appointed in the church first apostles, second prophets, third teachers; then deeds of power, then gifts of healing, forms of assistance, forms of leadership, various kinds of tongues.*

Once inside, you will meet many other laborers who Jesus has also called to the harvest. Maybe some of them are in need of fresh supplies themselves. Maybe they have become weary from the scorching sun and the parched land. Perhaps you are the one called to offer them refreshment. Can you offer the laborers help with the tools of Jesus—the tools of love, forgiveness, hope, joy, and humility? Maybe they need your support so they can go back to the field refreshed and ready to labor with renewed energy. Does your pastor, your priest, or the other members of your church need you to use the tools of Jesus for their healing? Maybe they need your support, your words of encouragement, and your prayers. We know they do not need our gossip, our judgment, or our condemnation, because those are the tools the Evil One uses.

Participating fully in the Church is never a one-way street. Yes, we receive much within her walls; however, we are also called to give to her. As Jesus taught us, we actually "receive" by "giving." A lesson we learned as children. It is better to give than to receive!

> *Luke 10:1-2 - After this the Lord appointed seventy-two others and sent them on ahead of him, two by two, into every town and place where he himself was about to go. And he said to them, "The harvest is plentiful, but the laborers are few. Therefore pray earnestly to the Lord of the harvest to send out laborers into his harvest."*

No matter how intense the elements, no matter how scorched the land or weary the laborers – you are promised victory. Everyone who opposes you will fall because Christ gives his laborers authority over all evil. All you need to do is labor for Christ. And yes, it will be work, labor is work. However, labor done well has its own rewards and labor done for Jesus promises divine rewards.

> Everyone who opposes you will fall because Christ gives his laborers authority over all evil.

Luke 10:17-20 - The seventy-two returned with joy, saying, "Lord, even the demons are subject to us in your name!" And he said to them, "I saw Satan fall like lightning from heaven. Behold, I have given you authority to tread on serpents and scorpions, and over all the power of the enemy, and nothing shall hurt you. Nevertheless, do not rejoice in this, that the spirits are subject to you, but rejoice that your names are written in heaven."

THE JESUS CODE CONNECTION
Member of the Infantry

HIS BRIDE

Remember, Jesus is a gentleman, and he will always respect your free will to choose him. He will not call you to work by his side unless you desire to do so. And like a true gentleman, he will sweep you off your feet and carry you away to his castle once you say yes— remember he has many castles. With your yes, you are invited into his church—his bride. The bride he died for.

Mark 2:19-20 - And Jesus said to them, "Can the wedding guests fast while the bridegroom is with them? As long as they have the bridegroom with them, they cannot fast. The days will come, when the bridegroom is taken away from them, and then they will fast in that day."

God promised to never leave his church. As a matter of fact, he gave his only son so she could fully live. Yes, she has suffered wounds while living in the world, how could she not? Who could sustain the full attack of the prince of this world without picking up some battle wounds along the way? Especially when this prince wants nothing more than to destroy you. Jesus understands the trials she faces, and he loves her beyond all measure. Yet the trials she faces, like the trials you face, hold the power to draw her closer to her bridegroom.

WHO IS THE CHURCH?

The church is Jesus's beloved, and she is made up of the children he died for. Yes, our church is made up of human beings who are subject to sin; however, Jesus desires her, and he is healing her. She is on display for all the world to see. The world has persecuted her with great vengeance, and she carries her pain forward. I know she has wounded many innocents, and I have personally heard some of their stories. She has been both perpetrator and victim. However, her wounds, like yours, provide her an opportunity to grow closer to her bridegroom.

> The church is Jesus's beloved, and she is made up of the children he died for.

Ephesians 5:25-26 - Husbands, love your wives, just as Christ loved the church and gave himself up for her, in order to make her holy by cleansing her with the washing of water by the word.

Perhaps you are being called to help the church so she can support those who seek the much-needed solace that can only be found within her walls. Maybe you are being called to help fortify her so she can become the bride Christ yearns for. We are all being called in some way. In my parish, we are seeing an increase in religious vocations: young men and young women giving their life to the church. I sit in awe as I witness the deep love they have for Mother Church and her children. Christ calls each and every one of us into his church for a purpose—so that she may become holy and pure.

> *Ephesians 5:27 - So as to present the church to himself in splendor, without a spot or wrinkle or anything of the kind—yes, so that she may be holy and without blemish.*

The transformation will happen; the church will be presented to her bridegroom in perfect splendor. God has already revealed this miraculous celebration to us in Sacred Scripture. The question now becomes, will you be at the wedding feast in the New Jerusalem? Will you join with Christ in the greatest celebration of all time? Will you partake of the celebration of this holy union? Will you say yes, will you become transformed, will you persevere and become cleansed so as to garner an invitation to this holy union? Many have already risen above their pain, many have already carried their cross, and many have already guaranteed their invitation, and they can show you the way. Our holy saints and our holy men and women that have gone before us lie await in service for you to call upon them. I hope to see you there my friend.

> *Revelation 19:7-8 - Let us rejoice and exult and give him the glory, for the marriage of the Lamb has come, and his bride has made herself ready; to her it has been granted to be clothed with fine linen, bright and pure—for the fine linen is the righteous deeds of the saints.*
> *- Revelation 19:7-8*

Revelation 19:9 - And the angel said to me, "Write this: Blessed are those who are invited to the marriage supper of the Lamb." And he said to me, "These are true words of God."

Revelation 21:2 - And I saw the holy city, the new Jerusalem, coming down out of heaven from God, prepared as a bride adorned for her husband.

THE JESUS CODE CONNECTION
Jesus' Bride – The Church

THE TRUE ETERNAL PROMISE

You are worthy of love. It is your birthright as God's child. And it is through perfect love, Jesus Christ, that you will experience freedom from all addictions, exclusion, and the powers of evil. However, in order to receive the fullness of your birthright, you must carry your cross and allow Christ to heal your pains. Remember, your birthright comes with admittance into your heavenly home, where there is no sin, no pain, and no more heartache. However, before you enter in, you must first receive the honor of experiencing the beauty of divine purification and transformation.

> In order to receive the fullness of your birthright, you must carry your cross and allow Christ to heal your pains.

Revelation 21:3-10 - And I heard a loud voice from the throne saying, "See, the home of God is among mortals. He will dwell with them; they will be his peoples, and God himself will be with them; he will wipe every tear from their eyes. Death will be no more; mourning and crying and pain will be no more, for the first things have passed away."

« Chapter 13 »

The 9th Face of Struggle: Mother as Nurturer and Comforter

Edith Stein - "We can do nothing ourselves; God must do it. To speak to Him thus is easier by nature for woman than for man because a natural desire lives in her to give herself completely to someone."

YOUR FATHER'S ROLE IN THE CHRISTIAN HOUSEHOLD

We are ending The Nine Faces of Struggle with the first heartache you experienced as a human being—separation from your mother. Her body supported you for nine months before your birth, and, hopefully, her arms held you for much longer. She is likely the one who provided most of the comfort and nurture you received in your childhood. However, before you can better understand your relationship with your mother, you must look at her relationship with your father.

While it may seem odd to begin a chapter on your relationship with your mother with a discussion on your father's role in your family, it makes perfect sense. A look at the creation of man reveals why. Regardless of which account of creation you read in the Bible, you will see that God made mankind both male and female to live a life together, and it is from this relationship that the first children were born. Further, God not only made Adam and Eve in his image, but he also proclaimed his creation to be "very good." While we can certainly never understand the mind of God, we can see that God chose to make mankind in his image in two distinctly different forms—male and female. One can only assume that within this creation we can find a fullness of love that is the image of divine love itself. In the second chapter of Genesis, we are allowed a glimpse into the relationship between the first man and the first woman— our first parents.

YOUR FIRST PARENTS: ADAM AND EVE

Adam, the first man, was created from dust, and after receiving the breath of life from God, he was placed in the garden to till and keep it. From the beginning, God created Adam to work and tend to God's creation. However, God noticed that Adam was alone and in need of a helper and partner. Then, both creator and the one created began a quest together. A quest in search for the perfect partner and companion for Adam. Side by side, God and Adam witnessed the world coming together beautifully as they sought such a creature. We can only imagine the delight that God and Adam must have taken in this most sacred and personal relationship in the garden. As God created every living creature, allowing Adam to name them all, they must have experienced real male bonding! You see, Adam was created to be in communion with God from the beginning. Adam's relationship with God is the relationship that will provide Adam with the greatest joy. God was Adam's first love, and Adam will always yearn for him.

However, none of the creations was a perfect mate for Adam. Adam needed a partner he could love and care for, one who was his complement and equal. God needed to create a very special creature for his beloved son, one that must be created differently than all others. God knew Adam needed a companion drawn from his own bones and flesh, one that he would love as he loves himself. It was out of love that God created Eve for his son Adam.

*Genesis 2:23-24 - Then the man said, "This at last is
bone of my bones and flesh of my flesh; this one
shall be called Woman, for out of Man this one was
taken. Therefore a man leaves his father and his
mother and clings to his wife, and they become one
flesh."*

We can only imagine the delight on Adam's face as he awoke and
first gazed upon this beautiful masterpiece and the precious gift
God had created specifically for him—his Eve. Adam's perfect
partner, created from his own body, must have been the loveliest of
all God's creations. She was born in the garden God had entrusted
into Adam's care. Her beauty perfectly complemented the rugged
Adam born of the dust. She would be the one to bring forth the
beautiful feminine love Adam's heart yearned for, and in return, he
would protect and care for her in his garden. Created from his own
body, Adam would forever desire to draw his Eve back toward
himself so he could care for her. Eve would forever desire to return
back home to Adam, seeking his love and protection. The two began
as one flesh, and as one flesh, God desired they remain, perfectly
complementing and caring for each other.

*Mark 10:6-9 - "But from the beginning of creation,
'God made them male and female.' 'For this reason
a man shall leave his father and mother and be
joined to his wife, and the two shall become one
flesh.' So they are no longer two, but one flesh.
Therefore what God has joined together, let no one
separate."*

THE JESUS CODE CONNECTION
Adam – Eve - Completeness

YOUR EARTHLY PARENTS

Much like Eve, your mother also needs her Adam—your father. She needs him to care for her so she can then in turn care for you. Your father is called, like Adam was called, to protect and provide for the Eve he chose above all others—your mother. And like Adam, your father is called to care for her as he does his own body—to the point of sacrificing himself for her if required. The love between a man and a woman is meant to reveal to the world an image of the fullness of God's love, a love that contains both the feminine and the masculine love of God. As a beautiful orchestra plays, the love between man and women reveals a completeness. A completeness that can only be fulfilled when God is found at the center of their love. As the masculine serves the feminine and the feminine follows the masculine, Adam serves his Eve and Eve follows her Adam.

> *Ephesians 5:25, 28-29, 33 - Husbands, love your wives, just as Christ loved the church and gave himself up for her . . . In the same way, husbands should love their wives as they do their own bodies . . . He who loves his wife loves himself. For no one ever hates his own body, but he nourishes and tenderly cares for it, just as Christ does for the church . . . Each of you, however, should love his wife as himself, and a wife should respect her husband.*

Your parents held these primal needs as well. Your father needed your mother for comfort, nurturing, and feminine love, and your mother needed your father for his protection, provision, and masculine love. Inside of their relationship your parents were uniquely suited to fulfill these needs for one another. However, sin entered into the world and as a result the love your parents experienced was likely limited, blunted, or perhaps vacant altogether.

The relationship your parents experienced likely failed to reveal the fullness of divine love God intended for them to share as a couple. The impetus of this limiting and blunting of love began before your conception. Heck, it probably began before your parents were born. It is important to acknowledge that the heartache your parents experienced in their relationship is something you cannot change. Remember, we can never change the past. All we can do is move forward and take the steps necessary so that love can heal the wounds the past left in its wake. Whatever your parents' relationship looked like, it is the relationship you were born into. Their story has left a significant imprint on your body, heart, and soul. And your mother's story, in particular, impacted your first experience with love.

THE JESUS CODE CONNECTION
Father – Mother – Needs

YOUR FIRST LOVE

You were created to love and to be loved in return. However, your humanity guarantees that you have experienced heartache along the way that limits your full experience of the love your heart desires. Undoubtedly, you have experienced hurt that has led you to create a wall of protection around your heart to one degree or another. Hurt that has perhaps been revealed in The Nine Faces of Struggle. This wall of protection likely started with heartache suffered in your relationship with your first love—your mother. Of course, this is not to say that your mother was bad. After all, most mothers deeply love their children. However, your mother's humanity

> However, your humanity guarantees that you have experienced heartache along the way that limits your full experience of the love your heart desires.

promises that she fell short of expressing love to its fullest and a long list of causes exist.

ROOT CAUSE OF THE "MOTHER WOUND"

Over the years, I have worked with many clients who have believed that they are unlovable and undeserving of love. I used to believe this about myself. They would "settle" for relationships with others where they were not valued, and they often found themselves the object of scorn, ridicule, judgment, or blame. These relationships included romantic relationships, employment relationships, friendships, relationships with their children, and even relationships with casual acquaintances. Of course, in the eyes of God, everyone is lovable and worthy of being treated with respect and love.

All of these clients held a similar pattern of life experiences with their mother. Some of the patterns I saw began in utero and continued throughout their life, moving well into adulthood. They believed at some level that their mother did not love them, that her love was conditional, and/or that her happiness was more important than their own. Sometimes they even felt guilty for being born, often believing they do not have a right to exist. For me personally, I believed that my mother's happiness was more important than my own and I denied my need for real love as a result.

Beliefs like these frequently find their primary root in a foundational belief that their birth, and often their life, was a burden to their mother. Such beliefs leave individuals sacrificing their own happiness in order that their mother may experience a better life. Victimhood can also play a role, as was the case in my own mother's life. Individuals can become trapped in the false belief that victimhood offers a pathway into love.

My mother, who also grew up in a troubled home, had polio in her teens. Looking back I can see how this experience impacted her view on receiving love. She always speaks fondly of the care she received at the hospital during her recovery. Being broken, being a victim, meant she would receive love and care – something she yearned for and didn't receive at home. This pattern entered into the relationship we shared, and sadly, blunted mother love from flowing as God intended. Through it all, for those who experienced a lack of mother love for whatever reason, there is a common thread: if the one who you first loved does not return your love, then how could anyone else ever love you? Those early "mother love files" are interwoven with your first neuropathways related to love. They became the lens you see love through and they become the foundation for all your love relationships.

Belief patterns like these all too often lead individuals into painful relationships where they are not valued and respected. While it may seem odd to others, painful relationships offer a type of comfort because they mirror their relationship with their first love—their mother. No matter how little sense these relationships make to outsiders, for those who experienced unrequited mother love, unhealthy unions can feel very comfortable. After all, we operate from our hearts and not our heads. What may seem illogical and irrational can make perfect sense to a wounded heart.

> What may seem illogical and irrational can make perfect sense to a wounded heart.

THE JESUS CODE CONNECTION
Mother – Bond

TRUTH AND COURAGE

In order to move into the life you want, it is important to look at your relationship with your mother through the lens of truth and courage. With truth and courage you can look at what she carried and the factors surrounding your relationship with her in a way that supports healing and transformation. You can experience transformation and not destruction in your relationship with your mother. Remember, you can turn around all old patterns with the right guidance and support, especially patterns that resulted from transgenerational entanglements. You can set a new pattern for your life and for the generations that follow.

QUESTIONS TO PONDER

I invite you to reflect on your mother's life through the lens of truth and courage. Remember, her story becomes a significant part of your story. In order to bring about needed healing in your life a survey of her trials and tribulations is vitally important. Did your mother experience any of the below-listed challenges? Or did she experience another challenge not listed here? If so, then it is highly probable that you experienced unrequited mother love at some point while growing up.

Obviously, the list provided here is not an all-inclusive list. It is, however, a list of common issues I have observed over the years when working with clients who suffer from a "mother wound." I invite you to reflect on the following questions, perhaps making notes in a journal and using these notes as you work through the next chapter, "The Language of LIVE."

- What was your mother's relationship with your father?

- What was her financial situation?

- Did she have extended family support?

- What was her health like?

- How many children did she have to care for when she became pregnant with you?

- Did she experience an abortion, stillbirth, or adoption of a child before you?

- Did you have siblings that needed extra care and attention?

- Did she worry a lot?

- Who did she turn to when she was struggling?

- Did she have a healthy relationship with God?

- What was her childhood like?

- Did she work outside the home?

- If so, was her work stressful?

- Was your neighborhood safe? Did she worry about your safety?

- What is her relationship with her own mother? Keep in mind that her experience with her mother may have been significantly different than your experience with your grandmother. Remember, when you met your grandmother, she was a different woman than the young woman she was when she was raising your mother.

- What challenges did your grandmother face that could have blocked or blunted her from expressing love to your mother? Remember, your grandmother was your mother's first love.

- What is your mother's relationship with her siblings?

> ### THE JESUS CODE CONNECTION
> *Your Mother's Wounds*

FALLING IN LOVE WITH YOUR MOTHER

Have you ever thought about how you fell in love with your mother and how this relationship, in turn, affected you and your ability to love all others? In utero, as a baby, and even as a very young child, you couldn't see where you ended and she began—the two of you were one in your mind and heart. When she experienced joy, your little body experienced joy; when she experienced heartache, your little body experienced heartache. Her life experiences and transgenerational entanglements left an imprint within you that you will carry throughout your lifetime. Before your birth, you never wanted to be separated from her, yet you did experience the heartache of such separation at a very tender age—your birth.

> Isaiah 49:5 - "And now the Lord says, who formed
> me from the womb to be his servant."

As we have already discussed, you were created to live in a community, and this community began with your mother. You likely lived the first part of your young life spending considerable time with her. As you grew, you turned to her for love, nourishment, and comfort. How she fulfilled these desires of yours played a significant role in your ability to love and be loved in return.

Sometimes a mother can give much, and this is beautiful for her relationship with her child—they are blessed indeed. However, there is much pain and heartache in the world, and many mothers cannot give their children the love, comfort, and nurture they desire from her for many reasons. Often transgenerational entanglements are found to be the core reason for such pain and heartache. Regardless of what your mother was able or not able to give you, you can become free to fully live the life your heart desires. You must face the painful spaces in your body, heart, and soul in order to transcend them and become happy and at peace. This includes facing the pain you experienced with your mother.

INTRAUTERINE BONDING

Have you ever looked at the smile on the face of a little baby and felt a sense of warm love? Aside from physical discomforts of hunger, pain, or perhaps a need for clean diaper, little babies are rather desirous of love. When you smile and speak lovingly to them, they return such affection with smiles and coos. As a baby, you too entered into the world ready to love and be loved in return. This ability to love began before you were born.

> As you grew in her womb, you shared the "love hormone" oxytocin with her.

At the moment of your conception, you received much from your mother. You inherited half of your DNA from her and all of the nutrients, biochemicals, and protection you needed directly from her body. As you grew in her womb, you shared the "love hormone" oxytocin with her. This hormone had a direct impact on your brain's ability to handle stress. If levels were healthy, you would experience a sense of belonging in the world. If they were low, as is the case of maternal and infant stress, then you became more prone to developing poor stress-handling capacities. Unfortunately, many children are born today in a state of adrenal fatigue as a result of maternal and fetal stress. When your mother was stressed, her body released the stress hormones and yours did as well.

Scent is also a powerful sense that significantly impacted the bonding you shared with your mother. You became familiar with the odor of your amniotic fluid in preparation for breastfeeding and physical contact with her. Even if you were bottle fed, evidence reveals that you likely preferred the scent of your mother above the scent of formula. When my children were babies, I remember the joy I felt kissing the top of their little heads, breathing in their sweetness as if it was yesterday.

During your time in the womb, your emotional body formed as well. Your brain synapses organized according to the emotional cues of your mother. These synapses would continue to develop after your birth in accordance with the environment you lived in. Your brain became hardwired, so to speak, to handle stress well or not. When your mother was happy and content, you felt happy and content; when she was brokenhearted, you were brokenhearted. You even responded to the sound of her voice so much so that you sought it immediately after your birth.

THE JESUS CODE CONNECTION
Mother – Child - Oneness

AFTER YOUR BIRTH

During your early life, you sought to continue this bond with your mother. How your mother responded to such seeking affected your ability to trust in love. If your mother experienced emotional pain in her lifetime and transgenerational entanglements then it is very possible that she couldn't fully bond with you prior to, or after, your birth as your heart desired—or even as her heart desired. Given the state of our planet, it is probable that your mother experienced heartache at some level that has, in turn, affected your relationship with her.

> If your mother experienced emotional pain in her lifetime and transgenerational entanglements, then it is very possible that she couldn't fully bond with you prior to, or after, your birth as your heart desired—or even as her heart desired.

As a young child, accepting the belief that your mother didn't fully love you as you desired was extremely painful. It was too painful to acknowledge, and you had to find a solution. This solution needed to affirm that your mom was "good" because she was the one you sought unconditional love from. Without her love, finding love in the world became virtually impossible because your relationship with her is where you learned what love looked like. The natural response in such situations was denial and a creation of a false reality.

In such false realities many children often believe that their mother's pain is their fault—a pattern that is frequently carried into adult life. If this pattern emerges in your life, it is important to recognize that your mother is doing the best she can do given the weight she carries. Likewise, your father is doing the best he can do given what he carries. Additionally, it is important to accept that whatever is going on in her life is not your fault and you cannot fix it. Her pain is hers to carry. Most often your mother's pain began before your birth, and given this, the solution to her pain must be found in the relationships it was created within. This is her work to do. Often her pain is found in her relationship with her parents and siblings. Remember, your mother can only pass on to you to you what she received.

UNREQUITED PARENT LOVE

As we have discussed in previous chapters, children hold within themselves a very deep need to belong and to be loved by their parents. To go to your mother, seek her love, and experience an absence or diminished love in return is something I call "unrequited parent love." If you have experienced unrequited parent love then you will likely sacrifice your own happiness, especially if you believe such sacrifice will lead your parents to happiness. A quick look at society and we witness this pattern.

Across all cultures and societies, we witness children seeking the love and attention of a wayward parent, an absent parent, or an abusive parent. Often in a similar manner, adult children seek to heal the emotional pains of their parents even if it costs them dearly. When such attempts are made and unrequited parent love is experienced walls are created around the heart. The walls are created in an attempt to not feel the pain of unrequited parent love. Unfortunately, these created walls will eventually serve to interfere with your giving and receiving love in other relationships in your life—whether you are aware of your walls or not.

These walls can be torn down and a new pattern established if you are willing to do the necessary work. We call this "positive pattern interruption." The impetus for positive pattern interruption is always found in God's love, which is accessed most beautifully when you make your relationship with him a priority in your life. Positive pattern interruption opens you to all the feminine (or masculine) love God has for each and every one of his children.

In the end, the journey will lead you toward acceptance of your mother for who she is and an honoring of what she has carried. Additionally, it will also call you to release any false beliefs that are not in alignment with God's plan for your life—false beliefs that interfere with giving and receiving love and forgiveness.

> *2 Corinthians 5:17 - So if anyone is in Christ, there is a new creation: everything old has passed away; see, everything has become new!*

THE JESUS CODE CONNECTION
New Path – Honor - Acceptance

THE REALITY OF MOTHER LOVE

While many suffer heartache when their mothers cannot easily love them, not all women are unable to bond with their children! If your mother experienced the life-giving emotions of love, hope, joy, and forgiveness during her pregnancy with you then your brain received the biochemicals associated with such emotions. If she felt safe and secure in her life, if she was protected and provided for by your father, her family, and his family, then her body beautifully created the biochemical picture congruent with well-being. You then became the beneficiary of this goodness in her life. Your brain developed in the milieu of love, contentment, safety, and security, and this will be the lens through which you naturally see the world.

With loving maternal experiences your brain likely seeks subsequent relationships that match these emotions throughout your lifetime. You will seek relationships with others who love and respect you and your behavior will foster the growth of healthy relationships naturally. Your mother's feelings toward her pregnancy, toward your father, toward her own mother, toward her friends, and toward God all play a part in your ability to give and receive love. If she was free to give and receive love, then she, in return, passed this on to you. If you are a child born into this type of family you have learned that it is safe to offer love to your mother, your first love, and from here you will find yourself offering love toward others in the world.

It is quite probable that your mother was somewhere in the middle while she was carrying you. Undoubtedly, she had heartaches that interfered with her ability to fully love you and this hurt your heart. However, it is also likely that a part of her heart deeply desired to love you and she easily expressed this. Whatever she was able to give you it is important to know that the love she gave you is enough for you to experience life fully alive. She gave you life and with this gift you are free to choose love. Where your mother couldn't love God can and will fill in. A new pattern can be created, a pattern that God desires for your life.

Through it all, you can experience a new way, a way that heals and allows the expansion of feminine love, of mother love, in your life and your family. A new pattern can be established for yourself, for your mother, for your children, and for the generations that follow. A pattern where love flows easily and where brokenheartedness is no more. A pattern where you allow God to nourish and comfort you with all the love your heart desires, a love that heals the wounds and tears down the walls you have created around your heart.

> Isaiah 49:15 - "Can a woman forget her nursing child, or show no compassion for the child of her womb? Even these may forget, yet I will not forget you."

ADOPTION AND OTHER CHALLENGING LIFE CIRCUMSTANCES

There are several life circumstances I have not specifically discussed in this book that present unique challenges to individuals who have suffered and experienced them. However, due to their multifaceted nature, such discussion is beyond the scope of this book. These topics warrant a book all to themselves, a book I am sure to write in the future. Given their importance, I have offered a few helpful books in the Appendix section. Such life circumstances include the loss of your mother through death, adoption, teenage pregnancy, multiple abortions, abandonment, neglect, drug use, and abuse. If you or someone close to you has experienced circumstances like this I invite you to explore the books listed in the Appendix.

Even in light of difficult circumstances, it is important to grasp that real transformation is possible with the right support. If this were not true, then we would have to accept that pain, heartache, and evil have greater power than God himself. Of course this is not true. What is true is that paths riddled with heartache are going to undoubtedly yield challenges that many will not understand. I do believe that when great challenges present, God offers great support and grace. I have witnessed this over and over in my practice. A promise of heightened union with God is offered to those with painful life stories, yet the difficult journey to him must be traveled first.

> *Romans 8:28 - We know that all things work together for good for those who love God, who are called according to his purpose.*

WHERE DO WE GO FROM HERE?

First, I believe you are served well by becoming aware of the false belief patterns you have taken on as the result of your relationship with your mother and father. These beliefs block your ability to fully live. While this type of discovery is a complex process there are a few core false beliefs that arise often. I invite you to examine and journal some of the false beliefs you hold, and work through them in the next chapter, "The Language of LIVE." Remember, you are always loved and lovable in the eyes of God. There is nothing you could every say or do that has the power to stop God from loving you.

Commonly Held False Mother and Father Beliefs

- I'm not good enough. And/or, I'm not worthy of love.

- Girls (boys) are inferior (superior).

- I'm responsible for my mother's (or father's) happiness.

- No one would love me if they knew the truth about me.

- I cannot be happy or at peace until my mother (father) loves me.

- No one cares about my feelings.

- My needs are not that important.

- Other people have it worse, and therefore they are more deserving of love and attention.

- Women can't be trusted.

- Men are monsters.

- Only broken (ill, sick, helpless) people are worthy of help or love. Therefore, I must remain broken.

- No one will love me if I'm ugly, if I'm fat, or if I'm not smart.

- Since I am bad, I am not worthy of love.

- I have to be perfect before I am worthy of love.

- I have no right to happiness when others around me hurt.

- I cannot be happy until my mom (dad, sibling, child, etc.) is happy.

THE JESUS CODE CONNECTION
Awareness – Truth - Family

If you hold any of the above false beliefs, then I invite you to ask yourselves if this thought process is true in the eyes of God. If it is not true then the thief came and he has tried to kill, destroy, and steal your life—and probably your parents' lives as well.

You (and your parents) were created for more than this, and it's time for all of you to reclaim what is rightfully yours. Transformation can be found; however, you must take the steps necessary to make the change and step into new life.

Can you imagine living a life where there is peace in your soul, forgiveness in your heart, and acceptance of the truth that is your life? A life where you experience an abundance of mother love, father love, peace, joy, and forgiveness? This, and more, is what Jesus promises all who follow him.

> *James 1:17 - Every generous act of giving, with every perfect gift, is from above, coming down from the Father of lights, with whom there is no variation or shadow due to change.*

« Chapter 14 »

LIVE and The Enneagram

Verse

Sometimes you stumble upon something and it grabs you so intensely that it changes the direction of your path – often with power unknown to you before. Well, that's what the Enneagram did for me. As I shared with you at the beginning of this book, I am a healer. I am always seeking and searching, trying my best to follow the path God continually lays out before me in an attempt to be of better service to others. The introduction of the Enneagram into my LIVE work has been a game changer – and the primary catalyst behind the revision of this book. The marriage of LIVE and the Enneagram has been a transformational piece in my work. I had client once tell me that upon read the description of her Enneagram type she felt that it was "reading" her soul. Well, it doesn't really "read" your soul. However, it describes your inner voice with succinct clarity and fullness of breadth that no other "personality" typing system that I have ever come across does. As a practitioner, it helps to me better understand the internal voice of my clients so I can better guide them on their healing journey. For you, it will help you to better understand your personal spiritual journey. When combined with LIVE, both a spiritual signpost and a Godly catalyst for healing present.

I still remember the moment when I was introduced to the work of Father Richard Rohr. I was on my way home from a pilgrimage to Ireland with members from my parish. Which, by the way, was amazing!!! My dear childhood friend, who now lives in Germany, Laura, joined me. We were like two little girls again on the trip! Anyway... back to Father Richard Rohr. While sitting on plane on the flight home the lady next to me, a fellow parishioner, asked me if I had ever heard of Father Rohr or his work. I said no. Then, something in her eyes told me that she had experienced many trials in her life and she had found sought after respite in his work. So shortly after my return home I sat down at my computer and solicited the assistance of the "Google Machine". Boy was I excited to learn about his work! I immediately ordered several of his books, one of which was titled "The Enneagram: A Christian Perspective". And the journey into the Enneagram began.

« Chapter 15 »

The Language of LIVE Within The Nine Faces of Struggle

I Peter 1:8-9 - Although you have not seen him, you love him; and even though you do not see him now, you believe in him and rejoice with an indescribable and glorious joy, for you are receiving the outcome of your faith, the salvation of your souls.

Since you have read this far, I can only assume that you believe you were created to live a life of fullness beyond your human comprehension. Perhaps you have even had several ah-ha moments as you have read through the chapters. So now what? How do you pull this all together so that you can fully live? How does The LIVE Method work, and how can it change your life for the better now that you understand The Nine Faces of Struggle?

In this chapter, you will learn The Language of LIVE (LIVE Language). Additionally, you will learn how to use LIVE Language to perform Self-LIVE by creating your own transformational statements in the privacy of your own home or place of prayer. If you are going to engage in Self-LIVE I invite you to obtain a journal at this point, where you can record your thoughts and prepare your LIVE Language Transformational Statements.

THE LIVE LANGUAGE ROADMAP

LIVE – Love is Victorious Everywhere

Like every journey, you need a good road map. The journey toward happiness and peace is no different. This journey requires the healing balm of love, yet sometimes we are hurt and we find ourselves estranged from love, the one and only thing that can heal us. How do we then, during our darkest moments, move into love? How do we move beyond The Nine Faces of Struggle into life? How do we experience love when our hearts hurt, when we are burdened, or when we are filled with anger, fear, or shame? Yes, each and every one of us desires happiness and peace; however, sometimes we don't know how to get from point A to point B, and we need a road map.

First, we must remember that God wants all of his children to choose him and become part of the divine love affair that God and Jesus share. We are all invited to leave the world and enter into the sacred love that exists between the Father and the Son – the Holy Spirit. The space where there is no more sorrow, pain, nor heartache—only pure love. Like the little fish swimming in the ocean, we are immersed in Love.

> *John 17:25-26 - "Righteous Father, the world does not know you, but I know you; and these know that you have sent me. I made your name known to them, and I will make it known, so that the love with which you have loved me may be in them, and I in them."*

The LIVE Language road map serves to bring you into Love. As you use the road map, you will discover that your pain is a great signpost directing you home to God. We all start at different points on this divine road map. Some of us are in a town called "anger," others "grief," others "pride," others "sorrow," others "regret," others "unforgiveness," and so goes the long list of towns on the map.

Now enters Jesus Christ. He is already in each and every town, ready to guide you home to Love. When you follow him, when you surrender to him, you learn how to forgive, you learn how to

> Jesus as fully human reveals to your human nature the path into Love, and Jesus as fully God reveals it to you in perfect Love.

be of service, and you learn how to sacrifice yourself for others—the ultimate love. You start in your town, and Jesus then directs you to the center of the map—Love itself. Jesus as fully human reveals to your human nature the path into Love, and Jesus as fully God reveals it to you in perfect Love.

THE JESUS CODE CONNECTION
Going Home – Divine Roadmap

THE POWER OF THE WORD

To begin, I have found over the years that offering transformational statements affords a release of pain. This release appears very mystical in nature. While I concede that I don't fully understand why it works so well, I do acknowledge that we can never know the mind of God or the healing he offers his children. With that being said, we do know that words are powerful and that we have power in our tongue.

> *Psalms 19:14 - Let the words of my mouth and the meditation of my heart be acceptable to you, O Lord, my rock and my redeemer.*

> *Proverbs 18:21- Death and life are in the power of*
> *the tongue, and those who love it (those who love*
> *to talk) will eat its fruits.*

Additionally, we know that the Word is Christ himself, and given this, all power and life is available in it. Interesting enough, *word* has a history worthy of noting here. In Christianity, *logos* refers to Christ himself whereas *rhema*, a Greek word, refers to Christ's utterance or a thing said. While both have been translated into English as *word*, in the original Greek, there was a considerable difference. Here, *logos* was a sentence, a sequence of verbs. Regardless of how we read the meaning of *word*, we can acknowledge that there is power in the words we choose to speak. We have power and free will to choose words that are in alignment with God's will, with his Son, or not.

> *John 1:1-5 - In the beginning was the Word, and*
> *the Word was with God, and the Word was God. He*
> *was in the beginning with God. All things came into*
> *being through him, and without him, not one thing*
> *came into being. What has come into being in him*
> *was life, and the life was the light of all people. The*
> *light shines in the darkness, and the darkness did*
> *not overcome it.*

> *John 1:14, 16-17 - And the Word became flesh and*
> *lived among us, and we have seen his glory, the*
> *glory as of a father's only son, full of grace and*
> *truth. From his fullness we have all received, grace*
> *upon grace. The law indeed was given through*
> *Moses; grace and truth came through Jesus Christ.*

In the end, we are all accountable for our words, and we can use them for healing and transformation or we can use them to bring about further pain in our lives and the lives of others.

In the end, we are all accountable for our words, and we can use them for healing and transformation or we can use them to bring about further pain in our lives and the lives of others. The more we engage in life-giving words, the easier it becomes to speak such words. So together let's speak words of truth, love, and life.

Matthew 12:36-37 - "I tell you, on the day of judgment you will have to give an account for every careless word you utter; for by your words you will be justified, and by your words, you will be condemned."

TRANSFORMATION WITH THE LIVE METHOD

There exists a certain framework within LIVE Language that facilitates the transformation of pain into joy. Inside of this framework, you will utilize three components necessary for transformation. They include forgiveness, acknowledgment and surrender, and permission and acceptance. Being as specific as possible when creating the transformational statements is essential. Including specific names, emotions, places, and even your age at the time of the pain in your statements will all help support transformation.

The Three Components of LIVE Language

1. Forgiveness

2. Acknowledgement and Surrender

3. Permission and Acceptance

THE LIVE METHOD TRANSFORMATIONAL RETREATS

In Chapter 4, you learned about The LIVE Method—Extreme Family Constellations. You were introduced to The LIVE Method Transformational Retreats, and hopefully, you have a basic understanding of how they work. There are four essential components to the retreats that I will share with you here before we move forward.

Four Essential Components to

The LIVE Method Transformational Retreats

1. Prayer

2. Confidentiality

3. Service of One Another

4. Complete Surrender to Jesus Christ and the Healing Available to us Through Him

Personal heartaches and pain are shared by those in attendance with the sole desire to bring about healing and transformation through Jesus Christ. Given this, we must protect and honor the sacred work. Prayer, our greatest power and weapon, is offered throughout each retreat. Once the work is done, we do not talk about it again. This piece is essential because, remember, our words have power. Once we have done our part in the retreat, we leave everything in the hands of the Holy Spirit, acknowledging that what we could offer afterward does not compare to what the Spirit offers, and we could possibly hurt the transformation process.

Of course, sharing is optional during the retreats. Sometimes transformation and healing need to begin by simply being present and making yourself available to support the others attendees. I deeply believe that all who participate are honored to be a part of the work and all benefit from participating—myself included. I am continually humbled by the stories shared and the strength and courageous nature of those in attendance. When you witness pain in another, it is the broken Christ you are looking at. In like manner, when you help another heal, you participate in the healing of Christ's broken body.

> *Ephesians 2:18-22 - For through him we both have access in one Spirit to the Father. So then you are no longer strangers and sojourners, but you are fellow citizens with the saints and members of the household of God, built upon the foundation of the apostles and prophets, Christ Jesus himself being the cornerstone, in whom the whole structure is joined together and grows into a holy temple in the Lord; in whom you also are built into it for a dwelling place of God in the Spirit.*

THE JESUS CODE CONNECTION
Transformation – Community - Healing

SELF-LIVE

If you are engaging in Self-LIVE, I invite you to start by finding a comfortable place to relax, free of distractions. I invite you to create an altar or special place in your home where you can retreat as needed to spend time with God. Fill it with beauty. Place things like a Bible, prayer cards, flowers, and healing essential oils in the space. Frankincense and rose oils are great essential oils to use. One of my favorite places to engage in LIVE Language is in the perpetual adoration chapel at my parish.

LET'S BEGIN

I will use as an example in each component a fictional argument between two spouses, Pat and Chris. Pat, the "offending" spouse, acted in such a way that the "offended" spouse, Chris, experienced anger. You will see how such anger can be transformed with LIVE Language statements.

> *Romans 12:18 - If possible, so far as it depends upon you, live peaceably with all.*

Opening Prayer: Dear Father God, I come before you in all humility, surrender, and love in the name of your son Jesus Christ. I present myself before you as your child who has sinned before you and who wishes to heal from the pain of my sin. I ask for divine guidance, protection, and wisdom as I sit here with you. I ask that your healing love consume me so that I can move more deeply into your divine love. I ask that you look kindly upon me. I ask that the Holy Spirit come into my heart and mind and make them his own. I ask that Jesus Christ draw me deeper into the divine milieu of his love. Most of all, I desire to love you above all else. I proclaim that this time together is yours and yours alone. (While signing yourself with the cross.) In the name of the Father, the Son, and the Holy Spirit, amen.

FORGIVENESS

We devoted an entire chapter to forgiveness in this book, and for good reason. Forgiveness is the cornerstone of real transformation and healing. Jesus Christ himself authored forgiveness for us on the cross when he showed us the way to freedom. There exist three components to forgiveness in LIVE Language: Self-Forgiveness, Forgiveness of Others, and Giving Others Permission to Forgive You.

SELF-FORGIVENESS: AN EXPRESSION OF SELF-LOVE

Statement: "I forgive myself for believing _____."

You must love yourself before you can love others. While at first blush this statement may appear a bit cliché, it is an essential component to your emotional well-being. As we discussed earlier, it has been estimated that the average person experiences somewhere between 50,000 to 70,000 thoughts per day. While this number is up for debate, what is not debated is the fact that every human being has thousands and thousands of thoughts every day! Some of these thoughts are statements you say about yourself. Of these thoughts, some of them are true in the eyes of God, while others are lies planted by the Evil One with the sole intention of separating you from receiving all the glory God has for you.

> You know you are speaking truth to yourself when your thoughts are congruent with God's vision of who you are, a perfect and lovable creation.

You know you are speaking truth to yourself when your thoughts are congruent with God's vision of who you are, a perfect and lovable creation. You are his child, a child of the one true King, and therefore you are special, unique, and perfect just the way you are. Thoughts that are loving, kind, and compassionate toward yourself and others are thoughts from God, anything else is a lie and in need of transformation and release. Additionally, thoughts that find their root in God promote a sense of internal well-being, peace, and happiness, which you now know from earlier reading have a profound effect on your physical, emotional, and spiritual well-being.

Thoughts that are loving, kind, and compassionate toward yourself and others are thoughts from God, anything else is a lie and in need of transformation and release.

When your internal tape player repeats messages that are in alignment with God's vision, you experience thoughts of truth, life, and light. In the presence of Truth, every cell of your being exists in harmony with Love itself and is therefore divinely supported. Much like a lie-detector test, your body will not be deceived by wrong self-talk. This is why we are programmed to seek happiness and not heartache. As your internal tapes play words of truth, every cell of your body, heart, and soul experiences the vibration of God's love. In this environment, you become strong and vibrant. You then share this frequency with the world. In a nutshell, you can't send love into the world when you internalize words in opposition to love about yourself. Remember, thoughts are things, and given this, they profoundly affect you.

When your internal tape player repeats messages that are in alignment with God's vision, you experience thoughts of truth, life, and light.

Through forgiveness of false beliefs, you begin the internal healing transformation necessary so that you can become filled with the internal love God has for you. Remember, love and love's companion emotions cannot occupy the same space in your heart that opposing emotions hold. Love cannot be present when anger is in your heart. Peace cannot be present when fear is in your heart. Hope cannot be present when despair is in your heart. Either you have love in a particular space in your heart, or you have some opposing emotion. If you find yourself speaking internal words that are self-deprecating, mean-spirited, belittling, and even possibly hateful, I recommend you write those false beliefs down and begin with them first. They have no business in your heart, and it is time for them to go.

Common Self-Forgiveness Statements

I forgive myself for believing (IFMFB):

- IFMFB I am not worthy of love.

- IFMFB I'm not good enough (smart enough, pretty enough, thin enough, loving enough, etc.) for _____ (fill in what your heart desires).

- IFMFB I'm not good enough (smart enough, pretty enough, thin enough, loving enough, etc.) to have happiness (peace, love, a good marriage, a successful career, a loving relationship with my children, etc.)

- IFMFB I will never be good enough for (or "to have a") _____ (fill in what your heart desires).

- IFMFB _____ people are not worthy of love. (fill in the blank; sick, lazy, overweight, divorced, "bad," law breakers, perpetrators, etc.)

- IFMFB I can't be happy without my mother's (father's, etc.) love.

- IFMFB I can't accept my life the way it is.

- IFMFB I need a different life before I can be happy.

- IFMFB I can't live a happy life with the parents (boss, salary, children, spouse, life circumstances, etc.) I have.

- IFMFB I need him (her, them, this particular business or establishment, etc.) to change before I can be free and happy.

- IFMFB I have to hide who I am in order to be loved and accepted.

- IFMFB no one cares (loves, needs, wants, etc.) for me.

- IFMFB I always attract the wrong people in my life.

- IFMFB I am hopeless (unlovable, undeserving, less than everyone else, etc.).

- IFMFB I have to hide the ugly parts of who I am before I can be loved.

- IFMFB I have to deny the parts of me that hurt before anyone will love me.

- IFMFB I cannot forgive him (her, them, etc.).

- IFMFB I have to be right and another (name them) has to be wrong.

- IFMFB I have to be in control.

- IFMFB that if I am not in control, everything will go wrong.

Statements Helpful With Abuse

I forgive myself for (IFMF):

- IFMF allowing my sense of safety (well-being, joy, happiness, trust, etc.) to leave as a result of, or during, the abuse (attack, etc.).

- Note: In the case of violence, often, the perpetrator only intended to hurt you in the moment. They didn't give much thought to your future state of mind. It's time to reclaim your life.

- IFMF letting important parts of myself (my ability to love and appreciate myself, my self-worth, my dignity, etc.) leave during the abuse (attack, etc.), and I call them back to myself. I ask God to heal these parts of me and restore them as he desires so that I can experience heightened levels of his divine love (protection, comfort, nurture, etc.).

FORGIVENESS OF OTHERS: OFFERING GRACE

Statement: "I forgive _____ for _____."

Remember, to not forgive another person causes pain in *your* body, heart, and soul. Sometimes it is helpful to see the one who hurt you as the child they were when the pattern leading them to hurt you began. This person came into the world as a little baby, wanting to love and be loved in return, and something painful came into their lives that stopped the flow of love. Love is our natural state of being. Of course, as discussed in Chapter 8, "The 4th Face of Struggle; Forgiveness of Self and Others," this step does not require that you invite someone into your life that you believe will only hurt you again. All of us are accountable before God for what we do and do not do in this lifetime.

> Remember, no one hurts another person without first experiencing their own hurt.

As you move through life, you will experience pain and heartache. Such life experiences present to you an abundance of opportunities to extend forgiveness. Sometimes forgiveness is hard and you want to hold on to unforgiveness and the false sense of power and security it promises. There are likely many things you need to forgive others for. Remember, no one hurts another person without first experiencing their own hurt. Hurt people hurt others. Healed people love others.

When we offer forgiveness, we change the trajectory of the harmful effects of pain and heartache. We proclaim a new spirit and a new path. Simply speaking transformational words starts the process. If you find it hard to forgive, then there are a few steps you can take.

Steps for Breaking Unforgiveness

- Pray for the person or establishment you are trying to forgive.

- Ask God to help you see the situation from their point of view.

- Try to see the person as the young child who experienced the pain and heartache that led them to this behavior.

- Ask God to help you see the wounds they carry that led to their treatment of you.

- Remind yourself that they are doing the best they can in this life, given their life circumstances.

- Ask God to enter into your heart and help you forgive.

- Use the Foot of the Cross and Breath of Christ visualizations and lay your unforgiveness on Jesus's cross. (Exercise listed below in Acknowledgement and Surrender Statements.)

- Practice the *I Am Love Meditation.*

I AM Love Meditation

You can do this meditation anytime, and it works very well during moments of acute stress. You do not need to practice breath work or even try to focus during this meditation. You can do this meditation when you are in the middle of a busy activity or when you are at rest. All you need to do is repeat "I—Am—Love" continuously until you feel at peace.

You can use this meditation during those times when you need a quick rescue. You can also use it during times of relaxed meditation to soothe and balance your central nervous system. Using meditation to promote relaxation and balance will help put you in a state of relaxed calm. In this state, your body will then move into parasympathetic mode where it will heal and repair itself.

Why *I Am Love* Works So Well

Why does this apparently simple little three-word meditation work so well? To understand its power, we can look to sacred scripture. In Exodus we see that "I Am" is God's name, the name he gave Moses to give to his chosen people who he had rescued from Egypt. We also see that Jesus said it many times when referring to his fully human and fully divine nature.

> *Exodus 3:14 - God said to Moses, "I am who I am."*
> *And he said, "Say this to the people of Israel, 'I am*
> *has sent me to you.'"*

"I am" is also a defining statement that holds great power when you speak it. When you speak "I am," you are proclaiming something as truth. I am hungry, I am cold, I am happy, I am smart, I am pretty, I am _____ (you fill in the blank). So what happens when you say and proclaim "I Am Love"? Great things! All of the cells in your body agree with this statement because it is a statement of truth. You were created in the image of God who is all love, and given this, you are also love. Unfortunately, many have forgotten who they are. They have given way to false beliefs that cause themselves and others harm while entering into sin and separation from God.

Lastly, when you say, "I Am Love," you are also uttering "God God" over and over. God is both the Great I Am and Love. And like any loving parent, God will hear your call for him. Remember, he already knows what your heart needs before you call out to him.

> *Matthew 6:8 - "For your Father knows what you*
> *need before you ask him."*

GIVING OTHERS PERMISSION TO FORGIVE YOU: AN ACT OF HUMILITY

Statement: "I give _____ permission to forgive me for _____."

You might ask yourself, why do I need to give another person permission to forgive me? After all, what they feel is their business, isn't it? Aren't their feelings between them and God?

In essence, giving others permission to forgive you is an act of humility. It helps you to see things from the other's point of view. After all, it often takes two to tango. Even in the cases of abuse and attack, granting another permission to forgive you is helpful because this act helps free you of pain. Instead of projecting anger, betrayal, fear, or hate, you become available to project forgiveness, which in turn helps your heart heal. As always, if you find yourself suffering from deep, profound pain such as abuse and attack, I recommend moving forward slowly, giving yourself the time and space you need for transformation. Sometimes the best thing you can ask God for in such cases is an increase in your ability to forgive.

Remember, Jesus authored humility as well as forgiveness. When we surrender to humility and we acknowledge that we hurt someone (even if that someone is ourselves, by not being able to forgive another) we unite with Jesus's humility. We unite with the one who humbled himself even though he hurt no one. By uniting with Jesus, we allow him to heal the pain between us and another. We then participate in the healing of the Body of Christ.

> By uniting with Jesus, we allow him to heal the pain between us and another.

Ephesians 4:1-7 - I therefore, a prisoner for the Lord, beg you to lead a life worthy of the calling to which you have been called, with all lowliness and meekness, with patience, forbearing one another in love, eager to maintain the unity of the Spirit in the bond of peace. There is one body and one Spirit, just as you were called to the one hope that belongs to your call, one Lord, one faith, one baptism, one God and Father of us all, who is above all and through all and in all. But grace was given to each of us according to the measure of Christ's gift.

Common Permission/Allowing Statements

I give (fill in name, group of names, organizations, etc.) permission to forgive me for:

- my unforgiveness.

- my inability to forgive.

- the anger (fear, frustration, spite, resentment, etc.) I hold toward them.

- hating them.

- everything I have ever said or done that in any way contributed to the pain and separation between us.

- hurting them.

- believing I have to be right and they have to be wrong.

- not believing they matter.

- believing my anger toward them is good for me.

- my part in our relationship that caused either one of us harm.

Praying for the one who hurt you is one of the quickest ways to transform your heart. Something beautifully spiritual happens to your heart when you do this that cannot be explained.

Praying for the One Who Hurt You

- Ask God to bless the other.

- Ask God to bless your relationship.

- Ask God to transform the hurt.

- Ask God to help you love the other more.

- Ask God to help you to see things through the other's eyes.

- Ask God to help your heart become more fully united with God's heart.

- Ask that you decrease and God increase as a result of the pain.

    Matthew 5:44 - "But I say to you, love your enemies and pray for those who persecute you."

Example Scenario Between Chris and Pat

Statements for Chris:

- I forgive myself for believing that holding on to this anger toward Pat is a good thing for me.

- I forgive Pat for everything he/she has ever said or done that has in any way contributed to this anger.

- I give Pat permission to forgive me for being angry at him/her.

Prayer for Chris: Lord God, please bless Pat today and every day. Please bless the love between us and help it expand while transforming the anger between us into love. Please help me to see this situation through Pat's eyes and help me to become free of my own pride and ego. Please help me to love Pat more as a result of this anger so that my heart expands and more fully becomes united with yours. Please help me to decrease as you increase as a result of this life experience. In the name of the Father, the Son, and the Holy Spirit, amen.

THE JESUS CODE CONNECTION
Forgiveness – Self – Others – Release

ACKNOWLEDGEMENT AND SURRENDER

There are four components to Acknowledgment and Surrender that deal with the pain you are releasing: Call It Up, Locate It, Surrender It, and Turn It. Once forgiveness has changed your heart, you are then ready to move forward and release the pain. This step corresponds to Stage 5 in the Stages of Healing: Acceptance. Once accomplished, peace of heart is experienced, and the door is opened for the next stage of healing: Love Entering In.

Call It Up

Call It Up Statement: "I call up all of this pain (anger, hate, unforgiveness, etc.) from every known and unknown place in my body, heart, and soul, and I lay it at the foot of the cross."

Locate it

Locate It Statement: "I ask my soul to locate the original event when this pain (anger, resentment, lack of trust, etc.) came into my body, heart, and soul, moving through all space and time, and I ask God to heal that picture so that I can love more."

Surrender it

Surrender It Statement: "I surrender all of this pain (anger, hate, resentment, etc.) at the foot of the cross for Jesus to do with it what he wishes."

Turn it Around

Turn It Around Statement: "I ask that God, through Jesus in the Holy Spirit, and Mother Mary, come into this space and heal it, filling it with divine love (forgiveness, patience, hope, etc.). God, please turn my heart around so I can see things as you desire. I ask for healing of all the parts of myself affected by this pain so that I can love God more as a result of this life experience."

Note: I don't always invoke Mother Mary's intercession, especially if I believe the client is not open to her aid. However, her intercession is extremely powerful, especially when dealing with pain that needs comfort and nurture to heal. Invoking her aid is profoundly helpful when dealing with a "Mother Wound."

GETTING UNSTUCK

Sometimes deep pain and heartache require a little extra help. I have found over the years that the following steps can help tremendously.

Foot of the Cross Visualization

Find a quiet, peaceful place and have a seat. Cup your hands together and look at the palms of your hands. You can do this with your eyes open or closed. If you choose to close your eyes, simply allow your mind's eye to see the palms of your hand.

Visualize your pain floating above the palms. Allow it to take on whatever form, color, and size it wants too. Once you clearly see your pain, invite Jesus to appear before you with arms outstretched. Look at his eyes and notice if he has anything to say to you. Allow him to speak if he does have something to say to you. Then begin taking slow steps toward him in your mind's eye. Allow Jesus to see what is in your hands as you approach him. Once you are near him, place your pain in his sacred hands and watch him smile as he receives it. Thank him for taking your pain and bow before him—full prostrate if you wish. You can bow before him physically or in your mind's eye, whatever feels best. Then ask him to heal your heart and bless you.

Renounce and Rebuke

Sometimes we feel like we need to engage in a little spiritual warfare. After all, we are living in a spiritual battlefield here on planet earth. While not all pain in our lives warrants a spiritual battle, I have found the following statement very beneficial and I use them from time to time.

Renounce and Rebuke Statements: "I renounce and rebuke the anger (hate, resentment, words I have said or thought, etc.) in this picture that has in any way separated me from God. I proclaim that this life experience only serves to bring me closer to God, and I give God full authority over this life experience in the name of Jesus Christ."

> *Luke 21:19 - By your endurance you will gain your souls.*

Example Scenario Between Chris and Pat

Chris: I acknowledge the anger I feel toward Pat because he/she left me alone last night and went out with his/her friends. I call this anger up from every known and unknown space in my body, heart, and soul, and I lay it at the foot of the cross for Jesus to heal it. I ask God, through Jesus, in the Holy Spirit, and with Mother Mary, to enter into that space and heal it, filling it with divine spousal love and forgiveness.

THE JESUS CODE CONNECTION
Release – Surrender - Cross

PERMISSION AND ACCEPTANCE

Now that you have cleared your pain and asked God to fill it with goodness it is time to claim the future of your dreams and set a proper intention. After all, you don't want to move forward in your life repeating the same old pattern that got you into this mess in the first place!

Permission and Acceptance Statements

"I give myself permission to accept_____."

"I accept and take you as my _____ and all that this entails."

"You are the right _____ for me."

One thing to keep in mind at this point is the reality of your life circumstances and the reality of the family you were born into. Fighting against the life you have keeps you in a constant state of struggle. This fighting requires a lot of energy, energy that could be used elsewhere. Sometimes accepting the truth is hard; however, God will always give you the strength to accept the truth. Remember, he is close to the brokenhearted.

> Deuteronomy 30:14 - But the word is very near you; it is in your mouth and in your heart, so that you can do it.

Much like forgiveness, acceptance does not require that you allow yourself to remain in a toxic or harmful relationship. Acceptance does, however, allow you to move on into your life with a peaceful sense of calm while developing a deeper understanding of who you are.

Common Permission and Acceptance Statements

I give myself permission to accept (IGMPTA):

- IGMPTA that my mom (spouse, dad, brother, sister, aunt, uncle, etc.) is the right mom for me.

- IGMPTA that I can be happy with the life I have now, just the way it is.

- IGMPTA that God will continually give me all the divine maternal comfort and nurture my heart could ever need.

- IGMPTA that God will continually give me all the divine paternal protection and provision my heart could ever need.

- IGMPTA and see things differently.

- IGMPTA that I can experience greater love, happiness, and peace as a result of this life experience.

I accept and take you as:

- my mother (father, brother, sister, aunt, uncle, spouse, etc.) and all that this entails.

You are the right:

- mother (father, brother, sister, aunt, uncle, spouse, etc.) for me.

Example Scenario Between Chris and Pat

Statements for Chris:

- I give myself permission to accept that I can love Pat just the way he/she is and that he/she is the right spouse for me.

- I give myself permission to accept that my love for Pat will continue to grow exponentially.

THE JESUS CODE CONNECTION
Accept – New Life - All is Well

Closing Prayer: Thank you God for this time together. I acknowledge that you are the single source of all my healing and transformation. I give you all gratitude and thanksgiving for healing my hurts. Please hover over me and direct my path so that it leads perfectly to you. Please help me to be your servant, serving others in all humility as you desire. (While signing yourself with the cross.) I surrender all in the name of the Father, the Son, and the Holy Spirit, amen.

> *Hebrews 12:1 - Therefore, since we are surrounded by so great a cloud of witnesses, let us also lay aside every weight, and sin which clings so closely, and let us run with perseverance the race that is set before us.*

RECAP ON LIVE LANGUAGE

Forgiveness

- Of self.

- Of others.

- Permission for others to forgive you.

Acknowledgement and Surrender

- Call it up.

- Locate it.

- Surrender it.

- Turn it around.

Permission and Acceptance

- Permission to accept your life as it is.

- Accept and take in the truth.

- You are the right one for me.

> *Romans 5:1-2 - Therefore, since we are justified by faith, we have peace with God through our Lord Jesus Christ. Through him we have obtained access to this grace in which we stand, and we rejoice in our hope of sharing the glory of God.*

« Chapter 15 »

Where to Go from Here

Edith Stein - "On the question of relating to our fellowman - our neighbor's spiritual need transcends every commandment. Everything else we do is a means to an end. But love is an end already, since God is love."

OK, so here we are, the last chapter. I hope you have found inspiration, insight, and hope in this book. *Understanding The Jesus Code* has been growing in my heart for years, and I am thankful it landed in your hands. Hopefully you have learned more about yourself, others, and the world through it. Most importantly, I hope that your relationship with God, Jesus, and the Holy Spirit has deepened as a result of your engagement with my book—your book.

You have read, and hopefully contemplated on, a long list of challenges in your life. You have learned about The Nine Faces of Struggle and hopefully you now better understand yourself and others as a result. Most importantly, I hope you have learned about the power within yourself, a power that will give you all the happiness and peace your heart yearns for. This power is Jesus Christ and he is ready and waiting to draw you into himself. He not only has the power to take away all your pain and replace it with peace, but he also desires to do this.

> *John 14:27 - "Peace I leave with you; my peace I give to you; not as the world gives do I give to you. Let not your hearts be troubled, neither let them be afraid."*

THE HURTING WORLD

The world is still hurting; you are probably still hurting as well. There is still work to be done, and we are all called to work together to heal the broken body of Christ. While none of us can be everything for everyone, providing healing to all, Jesus Christ can, and he is the healer of the world. You and I are each invited into his body to become the healing piece that is uniquely set aside for us. Yes, God has given each and every one of us an important role in the salvation of humanity. Not only is our role important and needed, but we have also been given unique gifts for the job assigned to us. It doesn't matter what we label ourselves—Catholic, Lutheran, Methodist, Episcopal, Baptist, Evangelical, Non-Denominational Christian, Jewish, Buddhist, Hindu, Muslim, New Age, or just plain spiritual—we are all invited to become part of the Holy Body. All we need to do is say yes to Jesus Christ and allow his Holy Spirit to direct us home toward God.

Jesus understands the pain of the world. He not only ascended to the highest point of heaven, the right hand of Father God, but he also descended to the lower parts of the earth where humanity experiences its greatest pain and separation from God.

> *Ephesians 4:9-12 -* (In saying, "He ascended," what does it mean but that he had also descended into the lower parts of the earth? He who descended is he who also ascended far above all the heavens, that he might fill all things.) And his gifts were that some should be apostles, some prophets, some evangelists, some pastors and teachers, for

the equipment of the saints, for the work of
ministry, for building up the *body of Christ.*

Jesus left work to be done on earth. I guess he could have done all the healing once and for all when he was here. After all, he conquered sin when he died on the cross and rose again on the third day. Yet knowing mankind was not ready for the fullness of life he had to offer when he died on the cross, he left us with important tasks to complete. He also gave us the Holy Spirit to assist us in our journey. This spirit will reveal to us the truth we need for healing and transformation. Through prayer and perseverance, we will receive his constant aid. Remember, prayer is both our greatest weapon and our peaceful source of solace.

> *John 16:12-13 - "I have yet many things to say to
> you, but you cannot bear them now. When the
> Spirit of truth comes, he will guide you into all the
> truth; for he will not speak on his own authority,
> but whatever he hears he will speak, and he will
> declare to you the things that are to come."*

Many think we are entering into the End Times. Maybe we are, maybe we are not. What we do know is that suffering exists and there is work to be done in the world. God has his own timetable and we know God is the victor. Jesus walked the earth for forty days after his resurrection. He spent this time teaching his followers the divine road map to share with the world, a road map that will direct God's children home. Just prior to his ascension, Jesus assured us that, while we will not know the time of restoration, he will give the Holy Spirit to the world so that the ends of the earth may know Jesus and the healing he alone offers. Jesus will come back, just as he left in all his glory—of this we are assured.

> *Acts 1:6-11 - So when they had come together, they
> asked him, "Lord, is this the time when you will
> restore the kingdom to Israel?" He replied, "It is not
> for you to know the times or periods that the
> Father has set by his own authority. But you will
> receive power when the Holy Spirit has come upon*

you; and you will be my witnesses in Jerusalem, in all Judea and Samaria, and to the ends of the earth." When he had said this, as they were watching, he was lifted up, and a cloud took him out of their sight. While he was going and they were gazing up toward heaven, suddenly two men in white robes stood by them. They said, "Men of Galilee, why do you stand looking up toward heaven? This Jesus, who has been taken up from you into heaven, will come in the same way as you saw him go into heaven."

THE JESUS CODE CONNECTION
Your Love Matters

A FINAL QUESTION FOR YOU

Are you ready to fulfill your part in the Jesus story? If so, then your next step is to discover your own life fully alive—fully healed. You will know you are living life fully alive when you love every person in this crazy world 100 percent of the time—24/7. Until then, you have work to do. I'm right there with you. I'm trying to love others more fully as I walk this earth. Only one person can help you to love more and you know his name: Jesus Christ. The Holy Spirit will guide you toward God, through Jesus Christ, where all the love, happiness, and peace you have ever dreamed of exists. Jesus will share with you all the Father promises, including a path home.

> *John 16:14-15 - "He (the Holy Spirit) will glorify me, for he will take what is mine and declare it to you. All that the Father has is mine; therefore I said that he will take what is mine and declare it to you.*

It is up to you to take the next step toward the fullness of life that awaits you. I invite you to find your way to the Father in your church, in your family, and in your friends. I invite you to attend a The LIVE Method Transformational Retreat, engage in Self-LIVE, or schedule a private LIVE session. It's time to unlock the painful patterns holding you back from fully living the life God offers you. Together we can help the world heal, and this starts with transforming you and your family so that the generations that follow can experience the fullness of life. Now is your time to reclaim what is rightly yours as a son or daughter of the one true King!

> *John 14:3-4 - "And if I go and prepare a place for you, I will come again and will take you to myself, so that where I am, there you may be also. And you know the way to the place where I am going."*

Appendix 1: Resources

CAROLYN'S WEBSITE

www.CarolynBerghuis.com

A FEW OF CAROLYN'S FAVORITE BOOKS

Books on Physical Health

Peter J. D'Adamo, ND - *Eat Right for Your Type*

Daniel G. Amen - *Change Your Brain, Change Your Life (Revised and Expanded): The Breakthrough Program for Conquering Anxiety and Depression*

Sally Fallon and Mary Enig - *Nourishing Traditions*

Candace B. Pert, PhD – *Molecules of Emotion*

Anthony William - *Medical Medium*

James L. Wilson, MD - *Adrenal Fatigue – The 21st Century Stress Syndrome*

Books on Emotional Health

Dan B. Allender - *Healing the Wounded Heart*

Don Colbert, MD - *Deadly Emotions*

Stephan Hausner - *Even if it Costs Me My Life*

Gabor Mate – *When the Body Says No*

Bessel van der Kolk MD - *The Body Keeps The Score*

Nancy Newton Verrier - *Primal Wound* (on adoption)

Spiritual Books

The Magnificat – daily scripture readings and more

The Word Among Us - daily scripture readings and more

St. Teresa of Avila – *The Way of Perfection*

Cynthia Bourgeau – *The Wisdom Jesus*

Megan Don - *Falling Into The Arms of God*

James Finley – *Meister Eckhart's Living Wisdom*

Christopher L. Heuertz – *The Sacred Enneagram*

Thomas Merton, O.C.S.O – *The Seven Story Mountain*

Richard Rohr, O.F.M. - *Breathing Under Water: Spirituality and the Twelve Steps*

Richard Rohr, O.F.M. - *Everything Belongs*

Richard Rohr, O.F.M. – *The Divine Dance: The Trinity and Your Transformation*

Richard Rohr, O.F.M. – *The Enneagram A Christian Perspective*

Maribai Starr – *The Showings of Julian of Norwich*

Appendix 2: Scripture and Quotes By Chapter

Introduction: From Brokenness to Wholeness; The Choice is Ours to Make

2 Corinthians 9:8 - And God is able to provide you with every blessing in abundance, so that you may always have enough of everything and may provide in abundance for every good work.

Isaiah 65:20 - No more shall there be in it an infant that lives but a few days, or an old person who does not live out a lifetime: for one who dies at a hundred years will be considered a youth, and one who falls short of a hundred will be considered accursed.

Acts 17:28 - For 'In him we live and move and have our being'; as even some of your own poets have said, for we too are his offspring.' Paul of Tarsus.

James 1:22-25 - But be doers of the word, and not hearers only, deceiving yourselves. For if any one is a hearer of the word and not a doer, he is like a man who observes his natural face in a mirror; for he observes himself and goes away and at once forgets what he was like. But he who looks into the perfect law, the law of liberty, and perseveres, being no hearer that forgets but a doer that acts, he shall be blessed in his doing.

Luke 23:34 - Jesus said, "Father, forgive them; for they do not know what they are doing." And they cast lots to divide his clothing.

John 6:51 - I am the living bread which came down from heaven; if any one eats of this bread, he will live forever; and the bread which I shall give for the life of the world is my flesh.

Jeremiah 31:33 - But this is the covenant which I will make with the house of Israel after those days, says the Lord: I will put my law within them, and I will write it upon their hearts; and I will be their God, and they shall be my people.

Chapter 1: Complexities of the Modern Person

Isaiah 65:17 - For I am about to create new heavens and a new earth; the former things shall not be remembered or come to mind.

Matthew 22:21 - They answered, "The emperor's." Then he said to them, "Give therefore to the emperor the things that are the emperor's, and to God the things that are God's.

Luke 11:9 - And I tell you, Ask, and it will be given you; seek, and you will find; knock, and it will be opened to you.

1 Corinthians 3:16 - Do you not know that you are God's temple and that God's Spirit dwells in you?

John 14: 6-7 - I am the way, and the truth, and the life. No one comes to the Father except through me. If you know me, you will know my Father also. From now on you do know him and have seen him.

John 14:16-17 - And I will ask the Father, and he will give you another Advocate, to be with you forever. This is the Spirit of truth, whom the world cannot receive, because it neither sees him nor knows him. You know him, because he abides with you, and he will be in you.

Revelation 21:4 - He will wipe every tear from their eyes. Death will be no more; mourning and crying and pain will be no more, for the first things have passed away.

Psalm 107: 19-20 - Then they cried out to the LORD in their trouble, And He saved them out of their distresses. He sent His word and healed them, and delivered them from their destructions.

Psalm 118:5 - Out of my distress I called on the Lord; the Lord answered me and set me free.

Chapter 2: From Zero to Following my Hero

Ignatius of Loyola - "Act as if everything depended on you; trust as if everything depended on God."

2 Corinthians 8:2 - for in a severe test of affliction, their abundance of joy and their extreme poverty have overflowed in a wealth of liberality on their part." - "for in a severe test of affliction, their abundance of joy and their extreme poverty have overflowed in a wealth of liberality on their part."

Ezekiel 18: 14-17 - But if this man has a son who sees all the sins that his father has done, considers, and does not do likewise... but gives his bread to the hungry and covers the naked with a garment, withholds his hand from iniquity ... he shall not die for his father's sin; he shall surely live.

Colossians 1:15-16 - He is the image of the invisible God, the firstborn of all creation; for in him all things in heaven and on earth were created, things visible and invisible, whether thrones or dominions or rulers or powers—all things have been created through him and for him.

Matthew 19:14 - But Jesus said, "Let the little children come to me, and do not stop them; for it is too such as these that the kingdom of heaven belongs.

Matthew 13:24-29 - The Kingdom of Heaven is like a farmer who planted good seed in his field. But that night as the workers slept, his enemy came and planted weeds among the wheat, then slipped away. When the crop began to grow and produce grain, the weeds also grew. "The farmer's workers went to him and said, 'Sir, the field where you planted that good seed is full of weeds! Where did they come from?' "'An enemy has done this!' the farmer exclaimed. "'Should we pull out the weeds?' they asked. "'No,' he replied, 'you'll uproot the wheat if you do. Let both grow together until the harvest. Then I will tell the harvesters to sort out the weeds, tie them into bundles, and burn them, and to put the wheat in the barn.'

Proverbs 17:22 - King Solomon suggested that "a merry heart doeth good like a medicine.

Romans 12:2 - Do not be conformed to this world, but be transformed by the renewing of your minds, so that you may discern what is the will of God—what is good and acceptable and perfect.

Chapter 3: How to Live Fully Alive

Corinthians 8:2 - For in a severe test of affliction, their abundance of joy and their extreme poverty have overflowed in a wealth of liberality on their part.

Genesis 3:4-5 - But the serpent said to the woman, "You will not die. For God knows that when you eat of it your eyes will be opened, and you will be like God, knowing good and evil.

Genesis 3:9-10 - But the Lord God called to the man, and said to him, "Where are you?" And he said, "I heard the sound of thee in the garden, and I was afraid, because I was naked; and I hid myself.

1 John 4:4 - Little children, you are of God, and have overcome them; for he who is in you is greater than he who is in the world.

John 14:27 - Peace I leave with you; my peace I give to you. I do not give to you as the world gives. Do not let your hearts be troubled, and do not let them be afraid.

James 4:7 - Submit yourselves therefore to God. Resist the devil and he will flee from you.

Colossians 3:15-17 - And let the peace of Christ rule in your hearts, to which indeed you were called in the one body. And be thankful. Let the word of Christ dwell in you richly, as you teach and admonish one another in all wisdom, and as you sing psalms and hymns and spiritual songs with thankfulness in your hearts to God. And whatever you do, in word or deed, do everything in the name of the Lord Jesus, giving thanks to God the Father through him.

John 14:30-31 - I will no longer talk much with you, for the ruler of this world is coming. He has no power over me; but I do as the Father has commanded me, so that the world may know that I love the Father. Rise, let us go hence" Jesus Christ to his disciples prior to his crucifixion.

John 10:10 - The thief comes only to steal and kill and destroy; I have come that they may have life, and have it to the full." Jesus Christ.

Hebrews 1:4-6 - (Jesus) having become as much superior to angels as the name he has obtained is more excellent than theirs. For to what angel did God ever say, "Thou art my Son, today I have begotten thee"? Or again, "I will be to him a father, and he shall be to me a son"? And again, when he brings the first-born into the world, he says, "Let all God's angels worship him.

2 Corinthians 4:4 - Satan, who is the god of this evil world, has made him blind, unable to see the glorious light of the Gospel that is shining upon him or to understand the amazing message we preach about the glory of Christ, who is God.

Ecclesiastes 3: 1-2 - For everything there is a season, and a time for every matter under heaven: a time to be born, and a time to die; a time to plant, and a time to pluck up what is planted.

1 John 5:19 - We know that we are children of God and that all the rest of the world around us is under Satan's power and control.

John 14:12 - Amen, amen, I say to you, whoever believes in me will do the works that I do, and will do greater ones than these, because I am going to the Father.

Mark 10:52 - Go," said Jesus, "your faith has healed you." Immediately he received his sight and followed Jesus along the road.

Matthew 8:3 - Jesus reached out his hand and touched the man. "I am willing," he said. "Be clean!" Immediately he was cleansed of his leprosy.

Matthew 9:22 - Jesus turned and saw her. "Take heart, daughter," he said, "your faith has healed you." And the woman was healed at that moment.

Mark 5:29 - Immediately her bleeding stopped and she felt in her body that she was freed from her suffering.

Mark 3:10 - For he had healed many, so that those with diseases were pushing forward to touch him.

Matthew 8:16-17 - When evening had come, they brought to Him many who were demon-possessed. And He cast out the spirits with a word, and healed all who were sick, that it might be fulfilled which was spoken by Isaiah the prophet, saying: "He Himself took our infirmities and bore our sicknesses.

Mark 6:5 - And he could do no mighty work there, except that he laid his hands upon a few sick people and healed them.

1 Corinthians 12:5-11 - To one is given through the Spirit the utterance of wisdom, and to another the utterance of knowledge according to the same Spirit, to another faith by the same Spirit, to another gifts of healing by the one Spirit, to another the working of miracles, to another prophecy, to another the ability to distinguish between spirits, to another various kinds of tongues, to another the interpretation of tongues. All these are inspired by one and the same Spirit, who apportions to each one individually as he wills.

John 14:6 - Jesus said to him, "I am the way, and the truth, and the life; no one comes to the Father, but by me.

Revelation 21:3 - I heard a loud shout from the throne saying, "Look, the home of God is now among men, and he will live with them and they will be his people; yes, God himself will be among them."

Luke 6:19 - And the people all tried to touch him, because power was coming from him and healing them all.

Isaiah 42:16 - I will lead the blind by a road they do not know, by paths they have not known I will guide them. I will turn the darkness before them into light, the rough places into level ground. These are the things I will do, and I will not forsake them.

Chapter 4: The LIVE Method – Extreme Family Constellations

Saint Mother Teresa of Calcutta - "Kind words can be short and easy to speak, but their echoes are truly endless."

1 John 4:18 - There is no fear in love, but perfect love casts out fear. For fear has to do with punishment, and he who fears is not perfected in love.

Genesis 1:31 - And God saw everything that he had made, and behold, it was very good. And there was evening and there was morning, a sixth day

John 3:16 - For God so loved the world that he gave his only Son, that whoever believes in him should not perish but have eternal life.

Psalm 139:13 - For thou didst form my inward parts, thou didst knit me together in my mother's womb.

1 Corinthians 12:12 - For just as the body is one and has many members, and all the members of the body, though many, are one body, so it is with Christ.

Ephesians 4:16 - By whom the whole Body is fitted and joined together, every joint adding its own strength, for each individual part to work according to its function. So the body grows until it has built itself up in love.

James 5: 16, 19-20 - Therefore confess your sins to one another, and pray for one another, that you may be healed. The prayer of a righteous man has great power in its effects. My brethren, if any one among you wanders from the truth and someone brings him back, let him know that whoever brings back a sinner from the error of his way will save his soul from death and will cover a multitude of sins.

Chapter 5: The 1st Face of Struggle: Emotions – Creator of Disease?

Thomas Merton - "Love is our true destiny. We do not find the meaning of life by ourselves alone - we find it with another."

Isaiah 41:10 - Fear not, for I am with you. Do not be dismayed. I am your God. I will strengthen you; I will help you; I will uphold you with my victorious right hand.

James 1:19-21 - You must understand this, my beloved: let everyone be quick to listen, slow to speak, slow to anger; for your anger does not produce God's righteousness. Therefore rid yourselves of all sordidness and rank growth of wickedness, and welcome with meekness the implanted word that has the power to save your souls.

Hebrews 11:1-3 - Now faith is the assurance of things hoped for, the conviction of things not seen. Indeed, by faith our ancestors received approval. By faith we understand that the worlds were prepared by the word of God, so that what is seen was made from things that are not visible.

Ezekiel 18: 14, 17 - But if this man begets a son who sees all the sins which his father has done, and fears, and does not do likewise" "withholds his hand from iniquity, takes no interest or increase, observes my ordinances, and walks in my statutes; he shall not die for his father's iniquity; he shall surely live.

Ephesians 3:16-17 - I pray that, according to the riches of his glory, he may grant that you may be strengthened in your inner being with power through his Spirit, and that Christ may dwell in your hearts through faith, as you are being rooted and grounded in love.

1 Peter 5: 6, 7 - Humble yourselves therefore under the mighty hand of God, that in due time he may exalt you. Cast all your anxieties on him, for he cares about you.

Ephesians 4:26-27, 29 - Be angry but do not sin; do not let the sun go down on your anger, and do not make room for the devil." "Let no evil talk come out of your mouths, but only what is useful for building up, as there is need, so that your words may give grace to those who hear.

Philippians 4:6-7 - Have no anxiety about anything, but in everything by prayer and supplication with thanksgiving let your requests be made known to God. And the peace of God, which passes all understanding, will keep your hearts and your minds in Christ Jesus.

Isaiah 43:18-19 - Do not remember the former thing, or consider the things of old. I am about to do a new thing; now it springs forth, do you not perceive it? I will make a way in the wilderness and rivers in the desert.

Chapter 6: The 2nd Face of Struggle: The Seven Stages of Healing

Romans 5:3-5 - Knowing that suffering produces endurance, and endurance produces character, and character produces hope, and hope does not disappoint us, because God's love has been poured into our hearts through the Holy Spirit who has been given to us.

Matthew 14:27 - But immediately he (Jesus) spoke to them, saying, "Take heart, it is I; have no fear.

Ephesians 6:10 - Finally, be strong in the Lord and in the strength of his might.

Philippians 4:13 - I can do all things in him who strengthens me.

Matthew 18:10 - See that you do not despise one of these little ones; for I tell you that in heaven their angels always behold the face of my Father who is in heaven.

Add - John 17:22-23 – "The glory that you have given me I have given them, so that they may be one, as we are one, I in them and you in me, that they may become completely one, so that the world may know that you have sent me and have loved them even as you have loved me."

Ephesians 4:31-32 - Put away from you all bitterness and wrath and anger and wrangling and slander, together with all malice, and be kind to one another, tenderhearted, forgiving one another, as God in Christ has forgiven you.

Psalm 94:19 - When the cares of my heart are many, thy consolations cheer my soul.

Galatians 2:20 - I have been crucified with Christ; it is no longer I who live, but Christ who lives in me; and the life I now live in the flesh I live by faith in the Son of God, who loved me and gave himself for me.

Matthew 6:33 - But seek first his kingdom and his righteousness, and all these things shall be yours as well.

Psalm 34:18 - The Lord is near to the brokenhearted, and saves the crushed in spirit.

Genesis 4:7 - If you do well, will you not be accepted? And if you do not do well, sin is couching at the door; its desire is for you, but you must master it.

1 Corinthians 6:19 - Do you not know that your body is a temple of the Holy Spirit within you, which you have from God? You are not your own.

Romans 15:13 - May the God of hope fill you with all joy and peace in believing, so that by the power of the Holy Spirit you may abound in hope.

Isaiah 58:8 - Then your light shall break forth like the dawn, and your healing shall spring up quickly; your vindicator shall go before you, the glory of the Lord shall be your rear guard.

Matthew 11:29-30 - Take my yoke upon you, and learn from me; for I am gentle and lowly in heart, and you will find rest for your souls. For my yoke is easy, and my burden is light.

Matthew 19:14 - But Jesus said, "Let the little children come to me, and do not stop them; for it is to such as these that the kingdom of heaven belongs.

Matthew 16:24-26 - Then Jesus told his disciples, "If anyone would come after me, let him deny himself and take up his cross and follow me. For whoever would save his life will lose it, but whoever loses his life for my sake will find it. For what will it profit a man if he gains the whole world and forfeits his soul? Or what shall a man give in return for his soul?

Isaiah 53:5 - But he was wounded for our transgressions, crushed for our iniquities; upon him was the punishment that made us whole, and by his bruises we are healed.

Romans 5:12, 21 - Therefore as sin came into the world through one man and death through sin, and so death spread to all men because all men sinned... so that, as sin reigned in death, grace also might reign through righteousness to eternal life through Jesus Christ our Lord.

Hebrews 12:2-3 - Looking to Jesus the pioneer and perfecter of our faith, who for the joy that was set before him endured the cross, despising the shame, and is seated at the right hand of the throne of God.

John 17:22-23 - The glory that you have given me I have given them, so that they may be one, as we are one, I in them and you in me, that they may become completely one, so that the world may know that you have sent me and have loved them even as you have loved me.

Matthew 5:15 - Nor do men light a lamp and put it under a bushel, but on a stand, and it gives light to all in the house.

Chapter 7: The 3rd Face of Struggle: The Pain of Exclusion

Psalm 127:3-5 - Sons (daughters) are indeed a heritage from the Lord, the fruit of the womb a reward. Like arrows in the hand of a warrior are the sons (daughters) of one's youth. Happy is the man who has his quiver full of them. He shall not be put to shame when he speaks with his enemies in the gate.

1 Corinthians 12:27 - Now you are the body of Christ and individually members of it.

Romans 8:14-17 - For all who are led by the Spirit of God are children of God. For you did not receive a spirit of slavery to fall back into fear, but you have received a spirit of adoption. When we cry, "Abba! Father!" it is that very Spirit bearing witness with our spirit that we are children of God, and if children, then heirs, heirs of God and joint heirs with Christ—if, in fact, we suffer with him so that we may also be glorified with him.

Psalm 146:3 - He heals the brokenhearted, and binds up their wounds.

Romans 8:18 - I consider that the sufferings of this present time are not worth comparing with the glory about to be revealed to us.

Genesis 1:26 - Then God said, "Let us make humankind in our image, according to our likeness;..."

Genesis 1:27-28 - So God created humankind in his image, in the image of God he created them; male and female he created them. God blessed them, and God said to them, "Be fruitful and multiply, and fill the earth and subdue it..."

1 Timothy 5:8 - And whoever does not provide for relatives, and especially for family members, has denied the faith and is worse than an unbeliever.

1 Corinthians 13:4-7 - Love is patient; love is kind; love is not envious or boastful or arrogant or rude. It does not insist on its own way; it is not irritable or resentful; it does not rejoice in wrongdoing, but rejoices in the truth. It bears all things, believes all things, hopes all things, endures all things.

John 13:34-35 - "I give you a new commandment, that you love one another. Just as I have loved you, you also should love one another.

By this everyone will know that you are my disciples, if you have love for one another."

Matthew 18:12-14 - "If a man has a hundred sheep and one of them wanders away, what will he do? Won't he leave the ninety-nine others on the hills and go out to search for the one that is lost? And if he finds it, I tell you the truth, he will rejoice over it more than over the ninety-nine that didn't wander away! In the same way, it is not my heavenly Father's will that even one of these little ones should perish."

Genesis 2:24 - Therefore a man leaves his father and his mother and clings to his wife, and they become one flesh.

Proverbs 5:18-19 - Let your fountain be blessed, and rejoice in the wife of your youth, a lovely hind, a graceful doe. Let her affection fill you at all times with delight, be infatuated always with her love.

Ephesians 5:31 - For this reason a man shall leave his father and mother and be joined to his wife, and the two shall become one flesh.

Ephesians 6:2 - Honor your father and mother"—this is the first commandment with a promise.

1 Corinthians 12:22, 25-27 - On the contrary, the parts of the body that seem to be weaker are indispensable,... that there may be no division in the body, but that the members may have the same care for one another. If one member suffers, all suffer together; if one member is honored, all rejoice together.

Acts 2:39 - For the promise is for you, for your children, and for all who are far away, everyone whom the Lord our God calls to him.

Chapter 8: The 4th Face of Struggle: Forgiveness of Self and Others

1 John 4:1-19 - We love because he first loved us.

1 Corinthians 1:10 - Now I appeal to you, brothers and sisters, by the name of our Lord Jesus Christ, that all of you be in agreement and that there be no divisions among you, but that you be united in the same mind and the same purpose.

Romans 12:14 - Bless those who persecute you; bless and do not curse them.

Psalm 51: 3-4 - For I know my transgressions, and my sin is ever before me. Against thee, thee only, have I sinned, and done that which is evil in thy sight,

Isaiah 1:18 - Come now, let us argue it out, says the Lord: though your sins are like scarlet, they shall be like snow; though they are red like crimson, they shall become like wool.

Ephesians 1:7 - In him we have redemption through his blood, the forgiveness of our trespasses, according to the riches of his grace.

Chapter 9: The 5th Face of Struggle: Overcoming Childhood Wounds

Saint Teresa of Avila - "Let nothing disturb thee; Let nothing dismay thee: All thing pass; God never changes. Patience attains All that it strives for. He who has God Finds he lacks nothing: God alone suffices."

Jeremiah 17-19 - Ah Lord God! It is you who made the heavens and the earth by your great power and by your outstretched arm! Nothing is too hard for you. You show steadfast love to the thousandth generation, but repay the guilt of parents into the laps of their children after them, O great and mighty God whose name is the Lord of hosts, great in counsel and mighty in deed; whose eyes are open to all the ways of mortals, rewarding all according to their ways and according to the fruit of their doings.

John 3:17 - For God sent the Son into the world, not to condemn the world, but that the world might be saved through him.

Luke 18:27 - "But he said, "What is impossible with men is possible with God.""

Jeremiah 29:11-13 - For I know the plans I have for you, says the Lord, plans for welfare and not for evil, to give you a future and a hope. Then you will call upon me and come and pray to me, and I will hear you. You will seek me and find me; when you seek me with all your heart.

Ephesians 4: 13-15 - Until we all reach unity in faith and knowledge of the Son of God and form the perfect Man, fully mature with the fullness of Christ himself. Then we shall no longer be children, or tossed one way and another, and carried hither and thither by every new gust of teaching, at the mercy of all the tricks people play and their unscrupulousness in deliberate deception.

Chapter 10: The 6th Face of Struggle: Father as Provider and Protector

Thomas Merton - "The real reason why so few men believe in God is that they have ceased to believe that even a God can love them."

Psalm 34:18 - The Lord is near to the brokenhearted, and saves the crushed in spirit.

Exodus 20:12 - Honor your father and your mother, that your days may be long in the land which the Lord your God gives you.

John 4:23-24 - "But the hour is coming, and now is, when the true worshipers will worship the Father in spirit and truth, for such the Father seeks to worship him. God is spirit, and those who worship him must worship in spirit and truth."

Chapter 11: The 7ᵗʰ Face of Struggle: Anxiety and Depression

Romans 8:35-37 - Who shall separate us from the love of Christ? Shall tribulation, or distress, or persecution, or famine, or nakedness, or peril, or sword? No, in all these things we are more than conquerors through him who loved us.

Hosea 4:6 - My people are destroyed for lack of knowledge; because you have rejected knowledge, I reject you from being a priest to me. And since you have forgotten the law of your God, I also will forget your children.

Job 36:11-12 - If they listen, and serve him, they complete their days in prosperity, and their years in pleasantness. But if they do not listen, they shall perish by the sword, and die without knowledge.

John 16:22-24 - So you have pain now; but I will see you again, and your hearts will rejoice, and no one will take your joy from you. On that day you will ask nothing of me. Very truly, I tell you, if you ask anything of the Father in my name, he will give it to you. Until now you have not asked for anything in my name. Ask and you will receive, so that your joy may be complete.

Romans 8:6 - To set the mind on the flesh is death, but to set the mind on the Spirit is life and peace.

Psalm 96:11-12 - Let the heavens be glad, and let the earth rejoice; let the sea roar, and all that fills it; let the field exult, and everything in it. Then shall all the trees of the forest sing for joy.

1 Corinthians 12:4-7 - Now there are varieties of gifts, but the same Spirit; and there are varieties of services, but the same Lord; and there are varieties of activities, but it is the same God who activates all of them in everyone. To each is given the manifestation of the Spirit for the common good.

Proverbs 4:23 - Keep your heart with all vigilance, for from it flow the springs of life.

1 John 5:11 - God gave us eternal life, and this life is in his Son. Whoever has the Son has life; whoever does not have the Son of God does not have life.

John 4:14-15 – "But whoever drinks of the water that I shall give him will never thirst; the water that I shall give him will become in him a spring of water welling up to eternal life." The woman said to him, "Sir, give me this water, that I may not thirst, nor come here to draw."

Matthew 11:28-30 - "Come to me, all you who are weary and burdened, and I will give you rest. Take my yoke upon you and learn from me, for I am gentle and humble in heart, and you will find rest for your souls. For my yoke is easy and my burden is light."

Psalm 147:3 - He heals the brokenhearted and binds up their wounds.

Proverbs 12:25 - Anxiety in a man's heart weighs him down, but a good word makes him glad.

Ephesians 4:29 - Let no evil talk come out of your mouths, but only what is useful for building up, as there is need, so that your words may give grace to those who hear.

Chapter 12: The 8th Face of Struggle: Addictions, Religion and God

1 Peter 5:10 - And after you have suffered for a little while, the God of all grace, who has called you to his eternal glory in Christ, will himself restore, support, strengthen, and establish you.

John 10:14-16 - "I am the good shepherd. I know my own and my own know me, just as the Father knows me and I know the Father. And I lay down my life for the sheep. I have other sheep that do not belong to this fold. I must bring them also, and they will listen to my voice. So there will be one flock, one shepherd."

Ezekiel 36:26 - A new heart I will give you, and a new spirit I will put within you; and I will remove from your body the heart of stone and give you a heart of flesh.

Luke 15:6-7 - And when he comes home, he calls together his friends and his neighbors, saying to them, 'Rejoice with me, for I have found my sheep which was lost.' Just so, I tell you, there will be more joy in heaven over one sinner who repents than over ninety-nine righteous persons who need no repentance."

Psalm 73:26 - My flesh and my heart may fail, but God is the strength of my heart and my portion forever.

Song of Solomon 4:7 - You are altogether beautiful, my love; there is no flaw in you.

John 17:20-21 - "I do not ask for these only, but also for those who will believe in me through their word, that they may all be one, just as you, Father, are in me, and I in you, that they also may be in us, so that the world may believe that you have sent me."

John 8:31-32 - "If you continue in my word, you are truly my disciples; and you will know the truth, and the truth will make you free."

Hebrews 10:24-25 - And let us consider how to provoke one another to love and good deeds, not neglecting to meet together, as is the habit of some, but encouraging one another, and all the more as you see the Day approaching.

Romans 8:38-39 - For I am sure that neither death, nor life, nor angels, nor principalities, nor things present, nor things to come, nor powers, nor height, nor depth, nor anything else in all creation, will be able to separate us from the love of God in Christ Jesus our Lord.

Matthew 16: 17-19 – "And I tell you, you are Peter, and on this rock I will build my church, and the gates of Hades will not prevail against it. I will give you the keys of the kingdom of heaven, and whatever you bind on earth will be bound in heaven, and whatever you loose on earth will be loosed in heaven."

1 Corinthians 12:28-31 - God has appointed in the church first apostles, second prophets, third teachers; then deeds of power, then gifts of healing, forms of assistance, forms of leadership, various kinds of tongues.

Luke 10:1-2 - "After this the Lord appointed seventy-two others and sent them on ahead of him, two by two, into every town and place where he himself was about to go. And he said to them, "The harvest is plentiful, but the laborers are few. Therefore pray earnestly to the Lord of the harvest to send out laborers into his harvest."

Luke 10:17-20 - "The seventy-two returned with joy, saying, "Lord, even the demons are subject to us in your name!" And he said to them, "I saw Satan fall like lightning from heaven. Behold, I have given you authority to tread on serpents and scorpions, and over all the power of the enemy, and nothing shall hurt you. Nevertheless, do not rejoice in this, that the spirits are subject to you, but rejoice that your names are written in heaven."

Mark 2:19-20 - And Jesus said to them, "Can the wedding guests fast while the bridegroom is with them? As long as they have the bridegroom with them, they cannot fast. The days will come, when the bridegroom is taken away from them, and then they will fast in that day."

Ephesians 5: 25-26 - Husbands, love your wives, just as Christ loved the church and gave himself up for her, in order to make her holy by cleansing her with the washing of water by the word.

Ephesians 5:27 - So as to present the church to himself in splendor, without a spot or wrinkle or anything of the kind—yes, so that she may be holy and without blemish.

Revelation 19:7-8 - Let us rejoice and exult and give him the glory, for the marriage of the Lamb has come, and his bride has made herself ready; to her it has been granted to be clothed with fine linen, bright and pure"— for the fine linen is the righteous deeds of the saints.

Revelation 19: 9 - And the angel said to me, "Write this: Blessed are those who are invited to the marriage supper of the Lamb." And he said to me, "These are true words of God."

Revelation 21:2 - And I saw the holy city, the new Jerusalem, coming down out of heaven from God, prepared as a bride adorned for her husband.

Revelation 21:3-10 - And I heard a loud voice from the throne saying, "See, the home of God is among mortals. He will dwell with them; they will be his peoples, and God himself will be with them; he will wipe every tear from their eyes. Death will be no more; mourning and crying and pain will be no more, for the first things have passed away."

Chapter 13: The 9th Face of Struggle: Mother as Nurturer and Comforter

Edith Stein - We can do nothing ourselves; God must do it. To speak to Him thus is easier by nature for woman than for man because a natural desire lives in her to give herself completely to someone.

Genesis 2:23-24 - Then the man said, "This at last is bone of my bones and flesh of my flesh; this one shall be called Woman, for out of Man this one was taken. Therefore a man leaves his father and his mother and clings to his wife, and they become one flesh."

Mark 10: 6-9 - But from the beginning of creation, 'God made them male and female.' 'For this reason a man shall leave his father and mother and be joined to his wife, and the two shall become one flesh.' So they are no longer two, but one flesh. Therefore what God has joined together, let no one separate.

Ephesians 5:25, 28-29, 33 - Husbands, love your wives, just as Christ loved the church and gave himself up for her, ...In the same way, husbands should love their wives as they do their own bodies.... He who loves his wife loves himself. For no one ever hates his own body, but he nourishes and tenderly cares for it, just as Christ does for the church, ... Each of you, however, should love his wife as himself, and a wife should respect her husband.

Isaiah 49: 5 - And now the Lord says, who formed me from the womb to be his servant.

2 Corinthians 5:17 - So if anyone is in Christ, there is a new creation: everything old has passed away; see, everything has become new!

Isaiah 49:15 - Can a woman forget her nursing child, or show no compassion for the child of her womb? Even these may forget, yet I will not forget you.

Romans 8:28 - We know that all things work together for good for those who love God, who are called according to his purpose.

James 1:17 - Every generous act of giving, with every perfect gift, is from above, coming down from the Father of lights, with whom there is no variation or shadow due to change.

Chapter 14: The Language of LIVE Within the Nine Faces of Struggle

I Peter 1:8-9 - Although you have not seen him, you love him; and even though you do not see him now, you believe in him and rejoice with an indescribable and glorious joy, for you are receiving the outcome of your faith, the salvation of your souls.

John 17: 25-26 - "Righteous Father, the world does not know you, but I know you; and these know that you have sent me. I made your name known to them, and I will make it known, so that the love with which you have loved me may be in them, and I in them."

Psalms 19:14 - Let the words of my mouth and the meditation of my heart be acceptable to you, O Lord, my rock and my redeemer.

Proverbs 18:21 - Death and life are in the power of the tongue, and those who love it (those who love to talk) will eat its fruits.

John 1: 1-5 - In the beginning was the Word, and the Word was with God, and the Word was God. He was in the beginning with God. All things came into being through him, and without him not one thing came into being. What has come into being in him was life, and the life was the light of all people. The light shines in the darkness, and the darkness did not overcome it.

John 1: 14, 16-17 - And the Word became flesh and lived among us, and we have seen his glory, the glory as of a father's only son, full of grace and truth. From his fullness we have all received, grace upon grace. The law indeed was given through Moses; grace and truth came through Jesus Christ.

Matthew 12:36-37 - "I tell you, on the day of judgment you will have to give an account for every careless word you utter; for by your words you will be justified, and by your words you will be condemned."

Ephesians 2:18-22 - For through him we both have access in one Spirit to the Father. So then you are no longer strangers and sojourners, but you are fellow citizens with the saints and members of the household of God, built upon the foundation of the apostles and prophets, Christ Jesus himself being the cornerstone, in whom the whole structure is joined together and grows into a holy temple in the Lord; in whom you also are built into it for a dwelling place of God in the Spirit.

Romans 12:18 - If possible, so far as it depends upon you, live peaceably with all.

Exodus 3:14 - God said to Moses, "I am who I am." And he said, "Say this to the people of Israel, 'I am has sent me to you.'"

Matthew 6:8 - "...for your Father knows what you need before you ask him."

Ephesians 4:1-7 - I therefore, a prisoner for the Lord, beg you to lead a life worthy of the calling to which you have been called, with all lowliness and meekness, with patience, forbearing one another in love, eager to maintain the unity of the Spirit in the bond of peace. There is one body and one Spirit, just as you were called to the one hope that belongs to your call, one Lord, one faith, one baptism, one God and Father of us all, who is above all and through all and in all. But grace was given to each of us according to the measure of Christ's gift.

Matthew 5:44 - "But I say to you, Love your enemies and pray for those who persecute you,"

Luke 21:19 - "By your endurance you will gain your souls."

Deuteronomy 30:14 - But the word is very near you; it is in your mouth and in your heart, so that you can do it.

Hebrews 12:1 - Therefore, since we are surrounded by so great a cloud of witnesses, let us also lay aside every weight, and sin which clings so closely, and let us run with perseverance the race that is set before us.

Romans 5:1-2 - Therefore, since we are justified by faith, we have peace with God through our Lord Jesus Christ. Through him we have obtained access to this grace in which we stand, and we rejoice in our hope of sharing the glory of God.

Chapter 15: Where to Go From Here?

Edith Stein - "On the question of relating to our fellowman - our neighbor's spiritual need transcends every commandment. Everything else we do is a means to an end. But love is an end already, since God is love."

John 14:27 - "Peace I leave with you; my peace I give to you; not as the world gives do I give to you. Let not your hearts be troubled, neither let them be afraid

Ephesians 4:9-12 - (In saying, "He ascended," what does it mean but that he had also descended into the lower parts of the earth? He who descended is he who also ascended far above all the heavens, that he might fill all things.) And his gifts were that some should be apostles, some prophets, some evangelists, some pastors and teachers, for the equipment of the saints, for the work of ministry, for building up the body of Christ.

John 16:12-13 - "I have yet many things to say to you, but you cannot bear them now. When the Spirit of truth comes, he will guide you into all the truth; for he will not speak on his own authority, but whatever he hears he will speak, and he will declare to you the things that are to come."

Acts 1:6-11 - So when they had come together, they asked him, "Lord, is this the time when you will restore the kingdom to Israel?" He replied, "It is not for you to know the times or periods that the Father has set by his own authority. But you will receive power when the Holy Spirit has come upon you; and you will be my witnesses in Jerusalem, in all Judea and Samaria, and to the ends of the earth." When he had said this, as they were watching, he was lifted up, and a cloud took him out of their sight. While he was going and they were gazing up toward heaven, suddenly two men in white robes stood by them. They said, "Men of Galilee, why do you stand looking up toward heaven? This Jesus, who has been taken up from you into heaven, will come in the same way as you saw him go into heaven."

John 16:14-15 – "He (the Holy Spirit) will glorify me, for he will take what is mine and declare it to you. All that the Father has is mine; therefore I said that he will take what is mine and declare it to you"

John 14:3-4 – "And if I go and prepare a place for you, I will come again and will take you to myself, so that where I am, there you may be also. And you know the way to the place where I am going."

Made in the USA
Monee, IL
17 February 2020

21934717R00164